Agenda 2030 – The Great Reset Exposed!

Our Freedom and Future in Danger?

NWO & WEF plans for 2022-2023

Hyperinflation – Food Shortage – Fuel Sortage

Rebel Press Media

Disclaimer

Decarbonization?

'Decarbonization = depopulation. Eliminating CO2 means eliminating the human race' - Period 2022 - 2024 will be crucial for all of us

CO2 is the "molecule of life" in our atmosphere. Without CO2, current life on our planet would not be possible. All climate propaganda notwithstanding - the level of CO2 in our atmosphere is still historically low (450-500 ppm), and is not far above the dangerous lower limit of 300 ppm. Below that level, everything that lives on this planet begins to die. So what a great idea of the West not only to significantly reduce CO2 emissions, but also to take it OUT of the atmosphere. In the US, a major project has now been launched to do exactly that. This is so absurd and dangerous, that it is more or less comparable to the scenario of well-known sf-movies in which an aggressive alien race 'terraforms' the Earth into another atmosphere, hostile to us, so that it becomes suitable for their form of life.

Expropriate farmers = attack on food supply

Entirely in line with Agenda-2030, in the U.S. huge numbers of farmers (directly or indirectly with Bill Gates' billions) are being forcibly bought out and thus expropriated (a process that has also started in the Netherlands now that the Parliament has agreed to it this year), after which their confiscated land will be partly taken out of the agricultural arsenal. The goal is to surrender total control over the soon to be severely limited food supply to the actually already functioning communist 'Great Reset' world government, although a number of countries (such as Russia) stubbornly refuse to submit.

The 'Heartland Greenway' project in Iowa is obviously presented as 'green' and supposedly beneficial to 'the climate' and 'the community', but as is the case these days with almost everything that the Western elite push through - think particularly of the Covid gene therapy injections - in reality the exact opposite is being achieved.

Once the project's infrastructure is up and running, the equivalent of the CO2 emissions of 3.2 million cars or three times of the city of Des Moines will be sucked out of the atmosphere and stored underground. On a U.S. scale, that's not much yet, but if successful, many more such plants are envisioned.

CO2 is food plants and crops, and therefore for us

Anyone who has finished elementary school knows that photosynthesis of plants and crops depends on sun, water and CO2. The greenhouses in the Westland are pumped full of CO2 to make the crops grow faster and bigger. It has made our little country one of the largest food exporters in the world.

Humans and animals, made of carbon, "consume" this CO2 after it has been converted by crops into proteins and molecules that are much needed by us. In the distant past, when there were thousands of ppm of CO2 in the atmosphere, our planet was one big green garden with huge rainforests where there are now deserts. With even less CO2 - essentially the 'God molecule' in our atmosphere - our planet will become even colder and drier, crops will fail en masse, and unprecedented famines will break out.

Those, as you know, are coming anyway starting next year, and that too is the direct result of the climate policies of the Western globalists. For years there has been a war on natural gas, which has now partially collapsed the production of fertilizer - on which the food of nearly 4 billion people depends.

Eliminate CO2 = eliminate humanity

If you want to remove all CO2 from the atmosphere - as Bill Gates has openly suggested several times, including in one of his infamous 'Ted Talks' of several years ago - then the Earth will become more or less a kind of second Mars and therefore completely unsuitable and uninhabitable for human life. Removing CO2 from the atmosphere therefore amounts to nothing more than 'genocide on a planetary scale', according to Mike Adams (Natural News).

'The war on carbon (/CO2) is a war on life. Against us. Decarbonization = depopulation. Eliminating CO2 means eliminating the human race.'

Once the project in Iowa is deemed successful, these plants will be built everywhere. CO2 will be sucked out of our atmosphere, causing plants and crops to shrivel and eventually die. Human civilization will be destroyed. If there is a little CO2 left, perhaps half a billion people can remain alive, as written on the 'Georgia Guidestones' (maximum 1.5 billion according to Agenda-2030).

Table of Contents

WHO Pandemic?

Gates ruefully acknowledges that current Covid injections 'cannot prevent infections' - U.S. Air Force loses 'war game' in which China invades under cover of biological attack

Bill Gates has 'asked' (= instructed) the West to put tens of billions into preparations (lett. 'Germ Games') for the next pandemic, which he believes could arise after the 'bioterror attack' announced by himself in 2020. In a recent interview, Gates suggested that that (likely false flag) attack will cause a pandemic with the deadly smallpox virus. That's why, according to him, a billion a year is needed for a special WHO pandemic task force, and why he advocates a (no doubt mandatory) 'patch' on your arm that would make constant re-injection a lot easier. That "patch" could also serve as a visible sign that you are obedient to everything the system demands of you.

Gates again announces next pandemic

'Bill Gates asks WHO to organize 'Germ Games' to prevent another pandemic,' Tech Times reported on November 4. That next pandemic, according to Gates, could be "worse" than Covid-19 (which is not so difficult, since that disease has been shown to be comparable in every way to a regular seasonal flu. Meanwhile, even Hugo de Jonge's CDA has admitted this). If it does not turn out to be the Marburg virus he mentioned earlier - for which the 'vaccines' would already be ready - the next p(l)andemic might consist of the return of a deadly variant of smallpox.

The Covid p(l)andemic should force humanity to put billions more into testing, 'vaccines' and other virus treatments, Gates said. He acknowledged that current Covid injections can't prevent infections, but "do help you with your health. (What that "help" for your health looks like in reality? Through mid-October approximately 50,000 official vax deaths and 1.5 million with serious long-term or permanent health damage in the West alone, numbers that statistical analysis suggests should be multiplied by at least 9 to 10 times).

Gates announced during his "Ted Talk" in 2015 an upcoming global pandemic, which eventually became a reality in 2020. That's why he wants one billion a year to be given to a pandemic Task Force of the (largely funded and controlled by him) WHO to organize 'Germ Games' so that the world is prepared for the next pandemic that is coming. 'If this pandemic doesn't convince you, the next one will,' the former Microsoft top executive grinned during a TV interview last year during the first phase of the corona crisis.

'What if a bioterrorist releases smallpox at 10 airports?'

'What if a bioterrorist releases smallpox at 10 airports?' With this question during the recent Policy Exchange interview, Gates is blatantly trying to incite new fears in order to not only extract additional billions to 'vaccinate' the entire world population over and over again, but also as an additional argument for handing over even more power to the UN and WHO's Special Pandemic Task Force (and thus to him).

In this context, is it mere coincidence that the U.S. Biomedical Advanced Research and Development Authority (BARDA) allocated $112.5 million in September for an oral smallpox treatment? Recall that the U.S. government and the Johns Hopkins Center conducted a "Dark Winter" simulation around a biological attack with the deadly smallpox virus back in June 2001. A recent war game simulation (early 2021) about a fictitious Chinese bio attack, which would precede a real invasion, did not end well for the United States.

BARDA, meanwhile, is also collaborating with BD (Becton Dickinson) in the development of a test that can distinguish Covid-19, influenza and other coronaviruses. Because the highly controversial PCR test cannot do this, it has been banned in the US as of January 1, 2022. Nevertheless, this PCR test is still being used in the Netherlands to report so-called "infections," which is an equally pointless and misleading exercise. For the same money, almost all of these so-called 'corona' patients simply have the flu.

Vaccination patch on your arm

During the interview, Gates suggests that 'vaccines' can also be used to eradicate the flu and even the common cold. 'We make vaccines just a little patch that you put on your arm, things that are incredibly useful even in the years when we don't have pandemics.' I underlined this, to emphasize the planned permanence of such a 'vaccine patch' on your arm, even if there were no more viruses (scientifically an absolute impossibility anyway, and even a highly undesirable condition because of the severe weakening of the human immune system).

It is quite conceivable that new 'patches' will keep on coming, and (via such a patch / vaccine patch) a technologically already developed quantum-dot tattoo will be injected just under your skin, creating a permanent 'sign' that will transmit via nanotech 'live' your vaccination status. That mark will be visible from the outside with an infrared scanner using a Luciferase enzyme, also injected.

Almost casually, Gates literally links the vaccination agenda to the climate agenda, a connection I have pointed out numerous times since the spring of 2020 by calling the events surrounding the corona/Covid pandemic a "coup by a globalist climate vaccination cult. In reality, it is one and the same agenda that must lead to a - de facto already functioning - communist world government that will be directed by globalists like Bill Gates and Klaus Schwab.

This "patch" also fits perfectly into the construction of the dreaded "sign of the Beast

I will not have to explain again that Gates' 'patch' fits perfectly into the global system of 'the Beast' that has been in the process of being established since 2020 as foretold in the Bible book of Revelation.

The dreaded 'sign of the Beast' has been injected into humanity little by little since late last year, the first two injections being a sort of 'MSDOS' test base for the coming 5G/6G/nanotech A.I. 'operating system' to which everyone will be mandatorily linked.

As more injections and booster shots follow (the EU has already ordered 6 booster shots for every citizen), the 'point of no return' is getting closer and closer. For vaxxers, refusal will soon be virtually impossible. The unvaccinated - as also predicted in Revelations - may eventually have to pay the highest price for their refusal.

According to investigative journalist Steve Kirsch, hospitals across the U.S. are being flooded with babies with serious heart problems caused by their mothers being injected with a Covid-19 "vaccine. And just like in Belgium, ICUs in America are bursting at the seams with sick fully vaccinated people. The wave of sickness and death feared by numerous scientists, experts and critical analysts as a result of this vaccination genocide now really seems to be taking hold.

Kirsch received a disturbing insider email about a children's hospital where all the NICUs (neonatal ICUs) are packed with newborn babies with serious heart problems. All of the mothers of these babies had themselves "vaccinated" against Covid completely. According to the author of the email, this information, which is very harmful to the 'vaccines', is also being suppressed. This is not surprising in a country where healthcare workers are fired if they refuse to be injected.

Doctors and healthcare workers confirm vax pandemic

The investigative journalist asked doctors and nurses if they could confirm the claims in the email. He received hundreds of responses. One of them said that several papers are now available confirming that the ICUs of many hospitals are 'packed' with sick and dying patients. 'The rooms are full of people with non-Covid symptoms...' The probable cause? Side effects of the vaccine.'

'How many newborn babies will soon be among them? The media and medical community will not tell you this. It will come from the common people who are fed up, and who are more afraid of the government than of Covid.'

Another wrote that it is now 'clearly established' that the number of spontaneous abortions has exploded since the injections began. 'My unvaccinated sister-in-law who just gave birth had been told by her doctor not to take a vaccine during her pregnancy because her last three patients had all miscarried right after their injection.'

In this context, someone pointed to a video of a (supposed) funeral director saying that he now gets many more dead babies than usual.

Pfizer and FDA knew risks, but approved 'vaccine' for pregnant women anyway

An official FDA approval report on the Pfizer 'vaccine' confirms that newborns of vaccinated women have high levels of (blood clots and thrombosis-causing) spike proteins in their organs. Pfizer had previously established this itself in tests on mice, and thus knew this in advance. Yet the same study was invoked to confirm the so-called "safety" of the Covid injection for pregnant women.

The U.S. CDC subsequently recommended that pregnant women - despite the almost complete absence of solid safety tests - be "vaccinated" against Covid. That decision was made based on a paper in the NEJM (New England Journal of Medicine), but it has since been retracted. However, the CDC did not adjust the advice, with far-reaching consequences: In addition to thousands of miscarriages, now sick and dead babies from vaccine-contaminated breast milk. and New England Journal of Medicine study: Covid injections kill 9 out of 10 babies in first trimester.

'My grandson was born this summer after a normal pregnancy and weighed over 8 pounds,' an official nurse responded. 'His mother was vaccinated during her 3rd month. He was in ICU for two weeks with 'breathing problems'. All tests were normal, but because of an 'unknown reason,' he had too little oxygen. I spoke to an ICU nurse who said that it is suddenly happening frequently this year, and there are also cases of babies with brain damage. However, she also said that no one is linking it to the mother's vaccination status. This is outrageous!

Yesterday we reported that the Covid 'vaccines' are also seriously damaging the health of unprecedented numbers of young people and core healthy athletes. A number of them have not survived their injections.

As long as real mass popular protests against these indirectly mandated dangerous gene manipulation injections fail to materialize, and almost everyone keeps meekly acquiescing to new Apartheid exclusionary measures, the number of - ever younger - victims of this vaxxicide will most likely continue to rise.

CEO: 'Either the vaccines don't work, or worse, the vaccines themselves cause Covid'

Kristiaan Deckers, medical director of the Antwerp hospital group GZA, has sounded the alarm because the full capacity for Covid patients in the ICU (25% of the total) is now full. 'The profile of our patients? They are now all vaccinated and have breakthrough infections. They are relatively young people between 55 and 60, quite a few of whom have immune problems. But they also see seriously ill younger people between 30 and 55, so the question is whether the vaccines are still working.'

'I know that sometimes one hears other rumors,' responded Dr. Jo Leysen, administrator of the AZ in Turnhout. 'But the vast majority of the patients we admit now are vaccinated people.' The commentator from ATV Antwerp: 'By the way, for those who would think that the hospitals are full of non-vaccinated people: that is no longer true.'

'Either the vaccines don't work, or they themselves cause Covid'

Other Belgian hospital officials wished to remain anonymous because, as in the Netherlands, openly reporting the real facts and figures will earn them severe reprisals. One CEO stated exactly what we suggested might happen last year: 'Either the vaccines don't work, or worse, the vaccines themselves cause Covid.

'But if we are publicly quoted, we lose our jobs and our profession. There is almost a cult-like zeitgeist in which no one is allowed to say anything about the vaccines, even if they don't work or harm people.'

Western politics and media keep up the lie

In Europe, politics and media continue to proclaim the 'pandemic of the unvaccinated' lie on a daily basis in order to justify ever more stringent QR-Apartheid measures designed to force everyone onto these life-threatening gene therapy injections that have proven to be a threat.

However, the harsh reality can no longer be denied: the 'vaccines' actually appear to seriously damage and weaken the immune system, something that critical scientists such as professor (em.) of experimental immunology Pierre Capel have been warning about in vain since last year. If these damages do not repair themselves spontaneously, a health disaster of unprecedented proportions will loom next year, especially if the injections are continued and booster shots are added.

An extremely dangerous cult

As our readers know, I myself have been talking for a long time about a globalist climate-vaccine cult that has taken over / forced obedience from our countries and governments. The term 'cult' was considered exaggerated by some people, but it is now becoming increasingly clear to others that we are indeed dealing with some kind of extremist sectarian religion.

Falsely packaged as "vaccines," experimental gene manipulation injections and their manufacturers have been declared, as if they were "gods" or "prophets," untouchable and sacred. Any form of criticism will get you increasingly severe exclusion sanctions, and if it were up to faithful cult members such as Ab Osterhaus, Hubert Bruls and the public broadcaster NTR, deportation or even death, whether or not by execution.

Do you remember the lessons at school about the Inquisition in the Middle Ages, when "witches" and other heretics were persecuted by the Roman Catholic Church, imprisoned and burned at the stake? And how the teacher told us that the barbaric times in which people who deviated from the norm for whatever reason were eventually massacred are definitely behind us after the Holocaust?

Food shortage?

Elite COP26 climate conference decides to cut energy, threatening to cause billions of starvation deaths - Only the power of numbers can stop this war on humanity

Aside from the affordability of our energy supply and thus our prosperity and well-being, the ideological war on fossil fuels that the 'Great Reset' / Agenda-2030 climate-vaccination globalists are waging will cause a guaranteed global famine as early as 2022 - 2023, which will kill at least hundreds of millions of people, and make food virtually unaffordable for billions more. Why this can be so certain? Because there is a huge shortage of fertilizer, which can only be made using fossil fuels. Western leaders are not only ignoring this, they are actually doing away with "fossil" at an accelerated rate.

Natural gas and other fossil fuels can be converted directly into ammonia (NH_3), which when combined with CO_2 or O_2 (oxygen) can be used to produce various types of fertilizer (Urea, nitric acid and ammonium nitrate). On the main chemical reaction (N_2 (nitrogen) + $3H_2$ (hydrogen) = $2NH_3$ (ammonia)) food production for about 3.8 billion people depends.

Wind and solar energy cannot be used for fertilizer production because natural gas (CH_4) is irreplaceable and not produced by 'green' sources. Therefore, limiting and discontinuing 'fossil' puts the survival of half the world's population at risk. In addition, the world's squeezing of oil, coal and other fossil fuels is already driving up prices sharply, fueling shortages and therefore unaffordable food.

COP26 elite decide on 'green' destruction of prosperity and well-being

Last week, 40 countries at the COP26 energy-climate conference decided to phase out coal in the coming years, which is a guaranteed recipe for global famines. A halt to coal will cause massive energy shortages, all while we already face a deliberately caused shortage of natural gas, which will not only monstrously increase energy bills next year, but also threaten to literally put countless people out in the (presumably extreme) cold this winter. Millions will literally have to choose between "do I turn on the heat today or make dinner?

Natural gas has already been made so expensive that 'the current price level no longer makes economically viable production possible,' warned SKW Piesteritz, Germany's largest fertilizer producer. In the U.S., Great Britain and Australia, too, fertilizer production has been partly halted because natural gas has become unaffordable as a result of the "transition" to a so-called "green" and "sustainable" society.

Read: our society is being deliberately and purposefully put under the green by making food and energy, and thus life itself, extremely expensive. The current fertilizer shortages-according to Free West Media partly caused by sabotage (such as an unusually large number

19

of accidents involving American freight trains) (2)-will cause catastrophic harvests as early as 2022, triggering large-scale famines and food riots.

Billions 'wiped out' by hunger, cold, disease, poverty, death and war

Add to that the crisis in the global supply chains, also orchestrated by Western climate globalists, the planned blackouts - in the emergency generators are already being installed in preparation, we have been told by a source - and the Covid 'vaccinations' imposed with ever harsher Apartheid measures, and the end result for the lion's share of the oppressed world population, including the Netherlands, is HUNGRY, COLD, SICKNESS, Poverty and DEATH, things that historically always lead to WAR.

We cannot stress enough that this is all demonstrably 'by design', planned and willed. Globalist governments and administrations have opened the frontal assault on humanity using food shortages, energy shortages, and pregnancy- and immunity-destroying gene therapy injections. The elite no longer need us because almost everything can be automated. This genocidal depopulation campaign, which was openly compared to the Holocaust by the inventor of the mRNA tech in the Covid 'vaccine's, is being sold to the common people as a 'necessary reset' because of a false CO2 'climate crisis' and Covid 'health crisis'.

Prince Charles literally called for a 'massive military-style campaign' at COP26 to bring about a 'fundamental economic transition' (= ALL power and wealth to a small elite club, the disenfranchised citizens who may survive own NOTHING more). British Prime Minister Boris Johnson urged the other leaders to 'take action on coal, cars, cash and trees', all under the guise of the anthropogenic CO2 'junk science' climate crisis theory.

Once billions of us have been "wiped out" by these methods and lies - Agenda-2030 wants to leave a maximum of 1.5 billion people, the Georgia Guidestones state a desired number of 500 million - these powerful banking families, billionaires and royal houses will have all the natural resources and the entire Earth to themselves for generations to come. The surviving slaves will be forcibly hooked up to a technocratic 5G/A.I. network, and can be controlled, abused and exploited at will, and eliminated as soon as they are no longer needed.

Only power of numbers can stop this war against humanity

Apart from a supernatural divine intervention expected by believers, the "power of numbers" is the only thing that can still stop this Third World War against the human race.

When billions of ordinary people finally put aside and accept their mutual differences, they can unite to put an end once and for all to the centuries-long rule of these evil families and their deceitful organizations (UN / WEF / EU / IMF / GAVI / Trilateral Commission, Bilderberg, BIS, Gates Foundation, Rockefeller Foundation, etc.), who are at most a few tens of thousands, but are making life an unspeakable hell for the rest.

That unanimity of black, brown, white, yellow, young, old, Muslim, Christian, Buddhist, Jew, vaxxer, unvaccinated, left, right or member of whatever letter of the identity alphabet, is the only thing these sadistic devils in human geeks fear, and is therefore exactly what they are trying to prevent with all their might with 'diversity' and things like QR/vax passes.

Do we fall for these flashy 'divide and conquer' tactics, or do we finally show that we have learned from the bloody oppression and other social tragedies of the past, which were so often the result of our unsuspecting blind faith in lying 'leaders' and 'governments'? Our complete survival may well depend on it.

Can we stop it?

The Golden Mean analysis: Indications that violence in Rotterdam was deliberately instigated by government agents provocateurs - Economist Armstrong: 'World population could collapse by at least 50% if everyone is vaccinated' - Are the agents of WHO/Bill Gates and WEF/Schwab already on their way to unleash the Marburg or smallpox virus to give us the final blow?

The violent images of the violent riots in Rotterdam went around the world. In numerous other countries there were also large-scale protests against the fascist vaxpas / lockdown tyranny with which almost all governments oppress their populations. The channel of the self-styled 'ethical political party' The Golden Mean (www.deguldenmiddenweg.eu), which has existed since March 2020, provides a crystal-clear analysis of the riots, pointing to strong indications that the violence was deliberately instigated by 'agents provocateurs'. It also urges the police to stand on the side of the people. But is there still time for that? Because the rapidly tilting mood in Europe may well make the WHO/Gates/WEF/Schwab elite decide to deal us the final blow with an iron fist as soon as possible.

Episode 157 of "Veritas Vos Liberabit" talks about two different groups that were active in Rotterdam. One group held an anti-2G/lockdown noise protest with pots, pans and whistles, among other things, and the other, dressed in black, protested against the fireworks ban on December 31. When fireworks were set off, the police / ME drove through with vans pretty hard. This was a trigger for the violence, and police cars were also vandalized and set on fire.

'Agents provoking?

'We reject all violence, but we also have to make a side note of that,' says Peter Baars. For example, in a side street of the Coolsingel there were piles of broken bricks ready to be thrown (a copy of what was done earlier in the US), So the question is whether the violence in Rotterdam was also 'instigated by agents provocateurs. If so, one can also wonder on which side these provocateurs are on.'

'A very black page in history is that the police... also fired at a number of people in a targeted manner. One of them got a bullet through his stomach. He was just standing there filming, according to many bystanders.'

These riots may have been provoked to get the public's disapproval for (new) demonstrations. 'Among the rioters, Romeos may have been hiding. This has happened more often than not. It gives rise to the declaration of emergency measures and perhaps a state of emergency, to draw even more power to the governments... We really have to take that into account.'

Eurogendfor agents seen and filmed: indication that riots have been provoked

Baars also points out that there are recordings of agents and men in black with truncheons bearing the emblem of the European organization of gendarmes (/marshals/ military police), Eurogendfor. An estimated 8,000 gendarmes are affiliated with it. Eurogendfor was created to put down riots in each other's countries. Reason: a Romanian gendarme will be prepared to shoot at men, but a military police may not be (and vice versa).

(Diederik Gommers has also acknowledged that 2G is not going to help, and that there is no difference between vaccinated and unvaccinated people. He also says it's going to take 10 years to restore the health care system destroyed by conglomerates. 'Why doesn't the government give the figures? writes Bert Brandsma in response to Gommers' statements (perhaps because then it will become apparent that here too the hospitals are flooded with vaccinated people?). Is Gommers indeed leaving the sinking ship, OR does he know that the Western regime is planning something much worse, and can he no longer stand behind it?)

Police and police leadership: say STOP!

Everywhere in Europe huge demonstrations are held time and again (even though they are virtually ignored in the mainstream media (= government propaganda channels)). In Austria it has even come to the point that the police are defecting to the demonstrators. They no longer feel like carrying out orders that are harmful to the Austrian people.'

Baars: 'My question to the police leadership is: when are you going to wake up?... When are you going to realize that the orders you are given are NOT in the interest of the people? When are you going to refuse to carry out orders that will ultimately place you on the wrong side of history?'

He therefore calls on the police leaders to say "BASTA!" to this government of "puppets" who only carry out orders from international organizations such as the WHO and the WEF. A different course must be taken, or else there will be a backlash, 'and the suffering will be incalculable and it will be complete chaos. So corps leadership, you should actually refuse to implement this anymore, and make it clear to the government that the C(ovid) measures must be lifted with effect from Monday.'

Only when everyone's voice is allowed to be heard and ALL the facts are on the table will the people, he says, be loyal to the conclusions that are then drawn. 'People who are not heard, who are trampled on, become distraught and start doing very crazy things. That's not a threat, it's a warning of what might be coming if we don't start turning this around.'

Economist Armstong: 'World population could collapse by 50% if everyone is vaccinated'

The riots in Rotterdam and large demonstrations in Australia, Croatia, Italy and Austria have not gone unnoticed by American economist Martin Armstrong either. French President Macron has now declared protesters 'terrorists', and is now deploying military anti-terror units against his own population. 'Anyone who still thinks this is about public health has no idea what you are standing behind. When have the most brutal rulers in 6,000 years of history ever put the entire society in lockdown for a disease? NEVER!

The U.S. CDC has acknowledged that there is no evidence that an unvaccinated person who has recovered can spread the virus. The vast majority of all new cases in hospitals are vaccinated people everywhere, 'and governments are pulling out all the stops to hide this.'

By forcing injections 'you actually lower the natural immunity. If you were really to vaccinate the whole world, you could unleash a collapse of the population by 50% or more... Just as the overuse of antibiotics has created superbugs, these vaccines will break down our natural immunity and increase the risk of new mutations coming.'

'Governments are using these vaccines to control the population, in preparation for Schwab's Great Reset, with which they are trying to accelerate the Fourth Industrial Revolution (actually 'Das Vierte Reich' - X.). They assume that robots will replace workers, so they need a guaranteed basic income. But they pray for drastic population reduction by at least lowering the birth rate' (and they might well do the same with these

Covid-19 injections. See our many previous chapters on this).

Will the final blow now follow even faster than thought?

Developments are moving so fast, that we may not even have months, but maybe only weeks, left to stop this Great Reset coup against our society, which will plunge us much deeper into a horrible totalitarian future with rock-hard oppression and zero comma zero freedom and participation.

I hope I am wrong, but I fear that the WHO/WEF globalists and their slave regimes (including those in The Hague) are about to strike with an iron fist and thus will try to deal the final blow. That blow or blows may consist of:

* The deliberate release of the (modified) Marburg and/or smallpox virus, as Bill Gates has already announced. All the more than justified doubts about corona/Covid will be wiped out once people die en masse. The Marburg/pox virus does not even have to be actually released yet, but can also be used for the huge wave of sickness and death that seems to have started everywhere as a result of the Covid injections.

* A Western false flag operation in Poland or Ukraine, or some other place, designed to provoke a supposedly "sudden" war with Russia. Historically, nothing distracts a people better than war. Such a false flag could also

consist of a days- or even weeks-long false flag 'cyber attack' blackout, which the WEF along with various governments have already practiced earlier this year (just as the same parties 'practiced' a global outbreak of a coronavirus in October 2019 (event201)).

* A series of natural disasters caused by HAARP energy weapons (no longer a conspiracy, but by now recognized and working) (e.g. a massive earthquake in the US, floods in Europe and China, etc.) that claim so many victims, that the chaos is seized upon for state-of-affairs and the permanent elimination of our last remnants of freedom.

Many are hoping that the governments will get cold feet and scale back their plans. I hope that these people are right, but given the enormous crimes of the past (almost) two years, the fact that 'our' leaders are willing to continuously lie so blatantly and to literally walk over corpses - if only by banning Ivermectin - gives me the niggling feeling that they will seize the events in Rotterdam and the uprising population for something horrible, and will not look at a few victims more or less.

Will the most inhumane dictatorship ever begin in 2022, or will we stop it?

Our future is literally hanging by a thread now. If the UN /WHO /WEF /EU /IMF /Gavi /BIS /Trilateral Commission (and you name the abbreviations) elite gets its way, then from 2022 onwards we will end up in the harshest and most inhumane dictatorship this planet has ever known, which as it now looks can make billions of victims. Agenda-2030 wants to reduce the world population to a maximum of 1.5 billion, which means that in the Netherlands about 14 million people will have to disappear.

Only a suicidal society will unwillingly agree to its own extermination. So resist peacefully (!) by, as Baars puts it, shutting down the entire country, and accepting nothing less than the complete and permanent removal of all 'C' measures.

And police and other order enforcers: should the regime in The Hague refuse to stop the step-by-step destruction of the economy, the sowing of fear and division, the imposition of discrimination and QR-Apartheid, and the damaging of public health with highly questionable experimental - and now acknowledged not protective - gene therapy injections, you might want to start thinking about putting together arrest teams that are ready to arrest and detain the decision-makers and executives in politics, institutions and media for their trial in a tribunal for high treason of their own people, and their already committed crimes against humanity.

Who still dares NOT make the comparison with WW2 / the Holocaust? - Australian freedom movement sends desperate SOS to the world: 'Help us, our country is lost'

It was announced last year, and now it is a fait accompli: the first Australians have been forcibly transferred to a concentration camp under the guise of an 'extreme public health threat' after 19 suspected Covid 'infections' were detected in the town of Binjari. The freedom movement 'Reignite Democracy Australia' recently sent out a desperate SOS to the world because 'our country is lost'. But who is to save Australians from this inhuman fascist tyranny? 'This is coming to Europe too, and they are doing everything they can to do this in North America too,' the American economist Martin Armstrong warned recently. You are still thinking: but not here, right? Think again: WHO/Bill Gates and WEF/Klaus Schwab have both the Australian and governments in their grip.

Residents of the villages of Binjari and Rockhole (220 and 130 inhabitants respectively) had already been placed in a strict lockdown, in which they were only allowed out of the house for necessary groceries, medical care, 2 hours of exercise, work and education (if it could not be done from home).

These 5 exceptions have now all been repealed, with the exception of emergency medical treatment. Also, everyone must get "vaccinated" as soon as possible. Minister Gunner justified the authoritarian measures with the glass-hard lie that "the danger to lives is extreme.

'So not a conspiracy theory after all'

38 'contacts' of the 19 'contaminated' people were tracked down and also transported by army trucks to the Howard Springs concentration camp (image not to be posted due to copyright). This has a total of 3000 places, officially for 'foreign' and 'domestic travelers'. Bernie's Tweets: 'So it wasn't a conspiracy theory after all.'

'Save us, our country is lost'

The freedom movement 'Reignite Democracy Australia' recently broadcast a desperate SOS to the world.

'Australia can no longer fight for itself,' Monica Smit said, pointing to the fact that protesters are being shot in the back, people are being arrested for social media criticism of the government and fired if they don't get injected, and even children are now committing suicide in alarming numbers. 'We are now a country of division, coercion and medical Apartheid... Our human rights are gone, gone!'

'We have been silenced. We have been attacked, blackmailed and psychologically damaged. We have tried to fight this battle alone, but the government has

instilled so much fear that we have lost the strength to
fight.'

'We are a broken nation, and although we will never
give up, we need your help to continue our struggle. We
need help from our international friends. We ask for
your support, to put political and economic pressure on
our leaders to change the destructive course we are on.
That is why we are organizing a worldwide protest, with
Australia excluded, in support of our freedom struggle.
This is an official SOS for my beautiful country. We beg
you to listen to our cry for help.'

'Our international friends', however, have ALL been
taken over by the same club of communist-technocratic
globalists. We are sorry, Australians, but we are faced
with the imposition of the same tyrannical dictatorship,
even if it has not yet been pushed through as far as you
have. (That's a deliberate divide-and-conquer
"patchwork" strategy. Many people still react with the
'head in the sand' argument 'Oh, but that's not with us,
it won't be with us, you know! Because the government
promised that!' (Just as they promised that there would
never be a vax passport, that vaccinations would never
be 'pushed', etc.).

'This is also coming to Europe, and they are doing
everything they can to do this in North America as well,'
warned American economist Martin Armstrong a few
days ago. 'With only 5 million (supposed) deaths due to
Covid worldwide out of a population at 7.8 billion, this is
the New World Order ending democracy!'

Who will deliver us from these enemies of humanity?

In WW-2 the Americans, British, Canadians and Australians came to deliver us from the Nazis. Now we need a new deliverance from a different kind of occupation. Now we need to be liberated from the WHO/Bill Gates, the WEF/Klaus Schwab, George Soros (= de facto European 'shadow president'), all their slavish political executives, the complex of Big Pharma and Big Banks, and certainly their all-powerful directors behind the scenes, especially the notorious Rothschild and Rockefeller families and just below them some of the best-known European and Eastern royalty.

This comparatively small club of elitists is throwing off all the masks of "humanity" and "democracy" at an ever-increasing pace, and in reality is showing itself to be a virulent enemy of humanity.

I abhor any form of violence, but apart from a supernatural / divine intervention hoped for and expected by many, the pressing question can be asked which country or countries have sufficient (military) power and political will to rid the world of these monsters and their institutions.

'Or are the reports of mysterious smallpox vials and procured medicines and vaccines just meant to keep the population in a constant state of fear?

Billionaire eugenicist Bill Gates announced with a grin last year that "if the first pandemic doesn't convince you" (to have you injected with gene manipulation "vaccines"), then the second will. A few months ago, he suggested that the next pandemic might be with the Marburg virus, but not long after, he changed that to a return of the dreaded smallpox. According to Natural News, the U.S. Biden administration is now poised to attack the entire global population with this "Angel of Death" bioweapon. In fact, in September, the government purchased millions worth of special smallpox drugs.

Already eight years ago, the federal government was stockpiling large quantities of smallpox vaccines. Now, all of a sudden, peculiar "smallpox" reports have appeared in the mainstream media recently. An employee of a lab in Philadelphia - owned by pharma giant Merck - allegedly stumbled upon 15 medicine bottles containing the smallpox virus somewhere in a refrigerator.

Then Bill Gates came up with the warning that "terrorists" (was he looking in the mirror at the time?) are planning to release a smallpox bio-weapon, and governments should therefore spend billions (on "vaccines" of course) to prevent "future pandemics.

Smallpox would have been eradicated by 1980. So why did the Biden administration slam the drug TOPXX, developed to treat smallpox, for $112.5 million in September?

'What if a bioterrorist releases smallpox at 10 airports?'

On November 7, we reported that Bill Gates has ordered the West to put tens of billions into preparations (lett. 'Germ Games') for the next p(l)andemic.

'What if a bioterrorist releases smallpox at 10 airports?' With this question during the recent Policy Exchange interview, Gates is blatantly trying to instill new fears in order to not only extract additional billions to 'vaccinate' the entire world population over and over again, but also as an additional argument for handing over even more power to the UN and the WHO's special Pandemic Task Force (and thus to him).

'These "germ-games" that Gates is talking about sound like false flag exercises to unleash "germs" (pathogens) on the world, and come at a time when we know that the globalists, in their sick minds, find it necessary to eradicate a large portion of the world's population,' All News Pipeline concludes.

Next pandemic: eradicated or a vaccine patch in your arm

So, after the pandemic 'exercise' Event201 (in October 2019) with the outbreak of a coronavirus became a reality just 3 months later, the next planned pandemic - whether with smallpox, a modified Marburg virus, or some other 'killer' (whether or not it really exists) - could soon be 'going viral' around the world.

Or are the reports of mysterious smallpox vials and procured drugs and vaccines just meant to keep the population in a constant state of fear? Another equally plausible explanation is that governments should be able to pinpoint some kind of 'false flag virus' once millions of people become seriously ill and/or die from the Covid injections, an extremely frightening but predicted by numerous experts development that has now begun.

The survivors of the coming plandemic should, if it is up to Gates (and thus the WHO = the real government), all be given a 'vaccination patch' in your arm, which may well be the completion of the foretold pricked 'sign of the Beast', with which all vaxxers are now gradually being integrated.

Slovenian head nurse resigns and shows journalists that vaccine bottles contain codes: 1 = placebo (for known figures), 2 = the mRNA injection, 3 = contains the ONC gene that would give everyone cancer within 2 years.

Old times have been revived and given a new look as hundreds of thousands of parents worldwide are willing to sacrifice their own children on the altar of the modern variants of Baal and Moloch. Pfizer's global war on children, who are abused as (so-called) human "shields" by injecting them with life-threatening experimental substances, - has now also reached Israel and Canada, where children as young as 5 are now being injected.

In many countries, millions of Europeans took to the streets in recent weeks to protest all the Covid measures, but without a mass readiness for action, such demonstrations are meaningless. By action we do not mean violence of course, but simply a full and firm refusal to cooperate with all these civil and human rights violating, freedom restricting and health damaging apartheid measures.

As is well known, I have been calling for this since last year. I therefore agree wholeheartedly with editor Brian Shilhavy (Health Impact News), who writes that 'I am sure that the globalist tyrants who are going full steam ahead towards their goal of forcing the world's population into slavery and reducing their numbers are laughing at you, since evidently none of you are addressing these tyrants.'

'No one is doing anything to save the children'

'As these protests grow in numbers and scope, children are being abused and potentially murdered in prisons, schools and churches,' he continued. 'I keep waiting for these huge crowds to leave the streets and go to these killing centers, which they could so easily close with such numbers of people. But all I see are videos of happy parents abusing and trying to kill their own children, brainwashed by a vaccination cult that devours their children. And no one intervenes to stop them and save the children.'

If you want to know what awaits a substantial (and perhaps even a very large) number of these young children, you need only look at some examples of children and adolescents who suffered serious health damage or died after being injected with these experimental gene-manipulation injections. Their parents are now horribly sorry, partly because many realize that they could have and should have known:

Only 'covidiots' refuse to sacrifice themselves and their children

I am a parent myself, and would consider any needle that even came close to my child, and also any obligation to do so, as a direct attempt at murder, and would therefore do everything in my power to stop it.

But apparently that makes me a wimp in the year 2021, and high priests such as Bill Gates, Anthony Fauci, Pope Francis and in my own country, for example, Hugo de Jonge and Ab Osterhaus, tell me that I should be happy that I am allowed to sacrifice not only myself, but also my child under the false guise of 'public health' to Big Pharma such as Pfizer and Moderna, the Baals and Molochs of our time.

What is it with the thousands of years old ineradicable fascination of people, peoples and complete religions with the sacrifice and (let others) murder of other people and even your own offspring in order to please the so-called 'gods', so that you yourself will get 'absolution' and perhaps a 'better life' (in this case regain your taken freedom)?

Slovenian head nurse: vaccine bottles contain codes

Let these people first inject themselves and their own children and family before they demand this of others (which, by the way, should never be an option anyway). However, an independent party should be able to guarantee that these well-known figures are not secretly given saline solution, as happened in 2009 during the swine flu outbreak in Germany, and according to a (presumed) head nurse from Slovenia is now also done on a massive scale in that country (and thus possibly in other parts of Europe).

40

This head nurse at the University Medical Center in Ljubljana resigned and told the camera that the Covid-19 'vaccine' vials would contain three codes. The vials with a code ending with a 1 contain a placebo, a saline solution, and are intended for well-known figures in politics, media, business*, etc.. They are not allowed to get sick and die, of course, because that would scare off the common people.

The vials marked with a 2 contain the mRNA vaccine, and in the vials marked with a 3, the ONC gene has been put in which stimulates under development of cancer. According to the head nurse, anyone who got "number 3" will develop cancer within 2 years. (2) (We have waited a while with this story, since there are very few direct sources available, and also it cannot be confirmed (yet) what exactly is said on the video).

(* Employees of BioNTech, Pfizer's partner, do not get inoculated with their own product anyway for "safety reasons". But for you it is apparently 'safe' enough to impose it on you under the threat of exclusion and other penalties...)

So hurry up and line up for your booster shot, because who doesn't want this?

Ivermectine?

After the Indian state of Uttar Pradesh (population 241 million) could recently be declared Covid-free thanks to

Ivermectin, now also Japan has defeated the flu-like illness with the help of this already decades known and proven safe medicine, which was strictly forbidden in the West precisely because it can end the p(l)andemic disease in a very short time.

The Big Pharma-controlled mainstream media, which since last year has condemned virtually all existing drugs that help proven Covid patients get back on their feet because politicians had simply designated 'the vaccine' as the only 'solution', of course claimed that wearing mouthguards and introducing vaccines had curbed Covid in Japan, and ignored the fact that all restrictive measures had not worked in a single country. In fact, shortly after the start of the injections, the number of dead and sick began to rise sharply everywhere.

In Japan, the number of casualties dropped dramatically after the director of the Tokyo Medical Association called on all doctors in late August to start dispensing Ivermectin (against the dictates of WHO=Bill Gates). Result? In the Japanese capital there were still 6000 (supposed) "cases" in August. By the end of September, there were only less than 100.

Press agency AP had to twist and turn to attribute the 'puzzling sudden success' in Japan to measures that had not worked, or had even been counterproductive, for more than a year. The directly demonstrable link with allowing Ivermectin was completely ignored.

Vaccine=Covid

On August 20, 2020, without vaccines, there were 832 new "infections"; a year later, there were 22,301, with nearly 70% of the population injected at that time. The average daily death rate was FIVE times higher than a year earlier. The number of positive tests (irrespective of the sense of the word) dropped from 25% in August to 1% in mid-October.

We predicted this last year, as did the false blaming of unvaccinated people for the growing wave of sick and dead, and the complete reversal of the facts in hospitals, where vaccinated patients are deliberately NOT allowed to be counted precisely because they are vaccinated, and the lie must be maintained that then you can no longer get serious Covid. The reality?

All over the world this is being observed by doctors and health care workers, but those who speak out publicly about it are almost all immediately suspended or fired, or quit themselves because they no longer want to cooperate with this monstrous deception (see also 11-10: Canadian ER doctor resigns: 'At least 80% of patients are fully vaccinated' and 25-08: Northern Irish hospital fires doctor after revealing that almost all seriously ill people are vaccinated).

CNN has recently had to grit its teeth and admit that the claim, adopted indiscriminately by the mainstream media, that Ivermectin is an 'anthelmintic for horses' and not suitable for humans is false. Ivermectin has been prescribed to millions of people for decades with great success and with hardly any side effects. So now Japan - which, thanks to the cautious administration of vaccines, has the 2nd lowest infant mortality rate in the entire developed world* - has a very safe and successful drug to combat the respiratory viruses such as influenza and corona that recur every winter.

(*This link has been demonstrated everywhere. Japan: 12 vaccine doses, infant mortality 2.79 per 1000 / Netherlands: 24 vaccine doses, infant mortality 4.73 per 1000 / United States: 26 vaccine doses, infant mortality 6.22 / 1000. In short: More Vaccines = MORE dead children).

Fellow men also cured by Ivermectin

Despite the fact that the treatment of Covid with Ivermectin is brutally suppressed (general practitioner is fined $ 150.000, customs intercepts packages with Ivermectin ordered abroad), here too people have been cured. Susanne Heijmans even lay terminally ill, but recovered completely after being administered Ivermectin.

The ANBB finds it astonishing that the NHG (general practitioners association) still issues a negative advice for Ivermectin despite the proven great success in dozens of countries, and requested the NHG on October 26 to adjust this advice to 'neutral'.

But politicians evidently do not want a healthy population and seem to continue to pressure the NHG. One of the important underlying reasons for banning Ivermectin in Europe is that the emergency authorization for the experimental Covid injections legally expires as soon as there are other proven effective drugs. The 'vaccines' may not be enforced from then on, and that is precisely THE goal.

Other experiences of Europe with Ivermectin, including the protocol of Dr. Zelenko (Bromhexine, Quercetin, vitamin D and C, zinc):

* Very sick woman from 1970 heals with Ivermectin, a 'shock in a positive sense';

* Drenthe couple (40 and 42, husband quite ill with high fever) cured within days with Ivermectin/Quercetin protocol);

* 56 year old man starts using Ivermectin in his third week of illness, then is better after 3 days;

* 17 year old sustained various health problems (including lungs) from corona (which this person had had in March) starting in October 2020; Started Ivermectin (and vitamins/supplements) in late July 2021, then recovered completely in a month;

* 80 year old grandmother got Covid in September, luckily already had Ivermectin and azithromycin in the house, which she started taking when she got a fever.

Already after 10 days she was walking with her grandchildren in an amusement park.

Husband cured woman: 'In Europe, other interests play a role'

* Heavily ill woman within 5 days 95% recovered thanks to Ivermectin. Her husband writes:

'I find it extremely shocking that a EU pharmacy, without reporting this to us, refused to make the promised medication (Ivermectin) available to us and that this did not cause any problem outside the Netherlands.'

'I have no faith in western 'medical science' and its policy of banning preventive or early treatment by GPs while outside the EU borders this is not a problem at all. I can only conclude that other interests play a role at interest groups and VWS, with the result that proper treatment of sick Covid-19 patients only starts with hospitalization. No wonder the hospitals are full.'

QR/vax card coup

Those (over)full hospitals are definitely not there yet, in my personal conviction exactly what the government seems to want*, because with that an extra (false) argument can be given to push through mandatory Covid-19 gene manipulation injections for everyone.

In addition, the local regimes are carrying out the EU's dictate to impose an unconstitutional QR code/digital ID on every citizen by the end of 2022, which will permanently do away with all our freedoms, rights and privacy. Ivermectin would mark the completion of this technocratic-communist QR code/vaxpas coup d'état being waged against our society.

The truth?

... or is this yet another diversion from the increasingly painful fact that it is the Covid injections themselves that cause mass illness and death?

Laughed off last year as a conspiracy theory of "wappies," but now openly acknowledged by the U.S. CDC: the SARS-CoV-2 coronavirus that allegedly causes Covid-19 is a chimera virus, and therefore can have been created solely and exclusively in a laboratory. Moreover, according to the CDC, this also applies to SARS-1, about which great panic was caused at the beginning of this century, but which also turned out to be a storm in a teacup. I wrote recently that the Chinese have known this for a long time and have interpreted SARS-1 as a Western biological attack. They would therefore have developed advanced, possibly already in progress, plans to overthrow the Western Rothschild-Rockefeller empire.

'Today, the Division of Select Agents and Toxins of the Centers for Disease Control and Prevention (CDC) published an interim Final Rule allowing SARS-CoV/SARS-CoV-2 chimeric viruses, resulting from some deliberate manipulation of SARS-CoV-2 to add nucleotides (acids) encoding SARS-CoV virulence factors, to the list of HHS select agents and toxins. In addition, the work to create this chimeric virus is a 'secret experiment,' and requires prior approval from the CDC before the experiment is conducted.

A chimera (virus)?

According to the Van Dale, a chim(a)era is an "animal or plant with genetic characteristics of two different races or species, which has been brought about by the artificial mixing of cells from two embryos respectively by grafting. (emphasis added). A Chimera (capitalized) is a 'fire-breathing (Greek) mythological monster, with lion's head, goat's body and snake's tail.'

The derivative related chimera is a 'dreamlike, chimerical'; chimerical is described as 'monstrous, chimerical. If anything has proven to be a chimera ('something that exists or is possible only in the imagination') in the past two years, it is the corona pandemic. Even the reputable British Medical Journal recently admitted that this 'pandemic' exists only on the TV screen and the corona dashboard.

And don't forget the R&D president of vaccine manufacturer Novavax, who acknowledged in front of the cameras of CNN that he did not have access to the Covid virus, but only had a digital model of it (!!!). This too was a 'wappie' conspiracy theory in 2020 and 2021, remember? All those 'Celebrities' on TV who thought they had to contribute to the unabashed sowing of hatred against the people who dared to claim anything other than that corona is a terrible killer virus, and that we should therefore all be injected with experimental gene manipulation substances ad infinitum, the often very serious consequences of which can never be undone?

Free research banned - what are scientists not allowed to discover?

The CDC has known from the beginning that the story about the coronavirus coming from a Chinese fish/meat market (the infamous bat soup) was pure nonsense. This again underlines the fact that all governments must have known about this as well, and thus the media deliberately spread a blatant lie about it throughout 2020. It is not for nothing that the CDC has now declared the research into SARS-1 and SARS-2 'secret' (restricted), so that special permission is now required.

The U.S. government wants to prevent scientists from finding out the true composition of these viruses, and thus from finding out who or where these artificial pathogens were created. Or perhaps find out that the government does not possess these viruses at all, and that they indeed only exist 'on paper'?

Of course Facebook immediately blocked the Wikileaks-Italy group that published this information, supposedly because it could cause 'physical violence'. And maybe that's right this time, because when millions of people wake up and find out that they've been massively conned by their own administrators and media, and they've been miserable for two years for absolutely nothing, it's not inconceivable that a people will want to take revenge for their screwed-up lives and futures.

'So world, what are you going to do about this?'

'So world, now that you know that SARS-CoV-2 was created in a lab, and now that you know that it was the government that funded the creation of SARS-CoV-2, triggering the Covid-19 outbreak that has killed millions, ruined entire economies and businesses, crushed people's personal finances, damaged children through social isolation - what are you going to do about it?" writes American radio host Hal Turner.

'Or is a bio-attack on yourself by your own government something that you will just let pass? Is the death of your family members from a government-funded virus something you just accept, without doing anything about it?

Now what if this bio-attack is slightly different, and the specific Covid-19 syndrome is not caused by a (supposed) virus, but by the injections themselves, as I suggested last year? (After all, the Covid syndrome-including the statistics-was seamlessly consistent with a regular flu, until large numbers of people had been injected, and suddenly more and more people were felled by thrombosis, brain hemorrhages, heart disease, autoimmune disorders, etc..

Planned popular uprising to pave way for world government?

And is Turner here calling for something that, according to some sources, the highest echelons of the globalist elite are actually aiming for, namely a worldwide mass uprising against the current governments, so that the chaos that ensues when they are forcibly removed is seized upon to present a world government as the 'saving grace'?

In other words: will the betrayers of their own people - by unscrupulous leaders who, as happened two days ago in Amsterdam, even go so far as to have peaceful demonstrators deliberately ambushed and beaten up by the M.E. - soon themselves be betrayed by their great masters behind the scenes? Are governments and parliaments now sacrificing their own citizens for Agenda-2030 / the Great Reset ('Build Back Better'), only to end up on the altar of sacrifice themselves, together with the big media leaders who have been spreading lies about important issues for years?

Let's hope that 'our' leaders will come to their senses in time and start siding with their peoples again, before it is definitively too late for both parties.

CEO: 'Huge, huge numbers are dying, mainly people aged 18 to 64' - *'Most are not claimed as Covid victims'* - *'A 10% increase would be a once-in-the-200 years catastrophe, let alone 40%'*

Top U.S. insurer OneAmerica has come out with a shocking news: the death rate for people belonging to the working population (ages 18 to 64) has risen by a staggering 40% from normal pre-pandemic levels. 'We are currently seeing the highest mortality rates in the history of this industry - not just at OneAmerica,' CEO

Scott Davison said at an online press conference. 'With every player in this branch, the data are consistent.'

OneAmerica (annual revenues $118 billion), headquartered in Indianapolis, has been around since 1877 and has the highest ratings in the insurance branch. CEO Davison emphasized that "huge, huge numbers" of people are dying, "primarily in the working age population of 18 to 64. When did that massive increase begin? In the third quarter, when most Americans had just had their Covid shots.

'To give you an idea of how bad it is: a three-sigma (statistical calculation), or a once-in-200-year catastrophe, would be a 10% increase over pre-pandemic levels. So 40% is unheard of.' Most claims made, by the way, are not for Covid-19 deaths, even though the U.S. government is operating the same demonstrated 'contamination' deception as in the Europe to report the highest possible number of Covid victims.

Vaxxicide

We reported very extensively last year on the many top scientists, doctors and other experts who warned of a huge wave of sick and dead as a result of the Covid gene manipulation injections. The graphene oxide nanoparticles and the spike proteins created by these "vaccines" go to all organs and cause autoimmune disorders, blood clots, brain hemorrhages, heart attacks and other heart diseases, among other things, which have now affected many hundreds of professional athletes worldwide, and are now felling more and more children.

It has now been widely scientifically demonstrated that the Covid 'vaccines' severely weaken the human immune system and permanently damage it in many. Booster shots', of which Minister Hugo de Jonge quickly purchased 6 - and which he would prefer to have injected into all of us - will therefore most likely be the final blow. In short: the vaccination genocide, or vaxxicide as we have been calling it for some time now, seems to have actually begun.

Deagel: 2/3 population in US and Europe gone by 2025

For years I have wondered why the military intelligence site Deagel - which we have covered a few times over the years - was so sure to report in its analyses that 1/3 to sometimes 2/3 of the population in the US and Europe will have disappeared by 2025. Also for the Netherlands, the (since this year taken offline) projections (in 2016) were frightening: our population would decrease by about 6.4 million people in the coming years:

Perhaps it was not a forecast at all, but an Agenda-2030 / Great Reset 'target', which our administrators are now trying to meet through the imposition and enforcement of life-threatening injections? It's a conspiracy theory, sure, but how many 'conspiracies' have turned out to be the truth since 2020 alone?

'Torches and pitchforks'

'I call for torches and pitchforks in 2022!" writes American radio host Hal Turner. And that, according to an unnamed billionaire in New Zealand, is exactly what would be the intention of the highest echelons of the globalist elite, namely that the enraged peoples - vaxxers who are getting sick and dying en masse, along with non-vaxxers who are seeing their countries deliberately destroyed - turn against their own governments in unison and call it off. The ensuing total chaos would then be used to present a "world government" that would restore order and end all misery.

It is not yet possible to say whether there is any truth to this 'conspiracy', but so far it is proceeding exactly according to the alleged scenario. In any case, the period 2022-2025 is going to be unprecedentedly intense, for everyone. Therefore, I wish all readers a SAFE New Year. And stay (as far as it lies within your power) HEALTHY - by now you know what you have to do to get there, and especially: what you have to leave out.

Smoke and mirrors?

End of 12,000 year cycle confirmed: 'The earth shall tremble from her place' (Isaiah 13) becomes a reality within 15 to 20 years (but possibly as soon as 2 to 8 years)

The signs in our own solar system are astounding: the 'black storm' on Neptune has been reversed; dwarf planet Pluto has lost 20% of its atmosphere in only 2 years time, and major changes in the famous 'red spot' on Jupiter show that the next cosmic wave movement of the electromagnetic 'galactic current sheet', which we discussed earlier, has not only arrived but is accelerating towards its climax. The protective magnetic field of our planet is now declining so rapidly that in 20 years at most, but most probably much sooner (2030 / 2025 or even earlier), it will be the end of the story for humanity. Note: this is no longer a 'conspiracy theory', but the unavoidable near future supported by scientific facts.

For some time now I have been following the YouTube channel 'Suspicious Observers', run by an academic who bases himself on scientific investigations by recognized researchers, who are regularly given the floor. A new, hour-and-a-half-long docu-film, 'The Earth Disaster Documentary', cites and summarizes key items from many dozens of previous videos. Although I have covered it more often (see, among others: Scientists warn of cosmic wave AND super solar flare in 2023 - (June 30)), there is now sufficient evidence to conclude that the 'end of the world', the 'Apocalypse', which has been wrongly predicted so many times, is now really very near.

At the turn of the century, NASA confirmed that the Earth's magnetic field had decreased by 10% in about 150 years. At that rate, it would be a long time before we were in trouble. But just 10 years later, European colleagues at ESA found that another 5% had disappeared in that very short time, and thus there was a gigantic acceleration. By 2020, the total decline was already at least 20%. There are clear indications that it is now going so fast that the magnetic field is losing 5% of its strength every year now or in the near future.

Tragically, we are going to see The Big One.

Tragically, we who are living now are the ones who will experience 'The Big One'," begins Ben Davidson, who in recent years has been subjected to a number of debunk attempts, but who is now rapidly being proven right by the latest research from systems scientists and professional journals.

The undulations of the electromagnetic "galactic current sheet," which we face every 12,000 years.

(According to him, the only reason this subject is called pseudo-science is mainly due to CIA agent Charles Hapgood, who for years posed as a professor, and managed to take centuries of studies and a wagon load of evidence off the table, and replace it with the now debunked prescribed scientific 'reality'. This was blatantly designed to keep the world's population ignorant).

Davidson talks about the end of the 12,000 year cosmic cycle after which the next 'end of the world' always occurs. 'And that's not science fiction. We are ALL the key players' of the 'disaster script' that we will experience in the coming years. 'And the sun is playing the role of the destroyer.' Davidson stresses that all the evidence points to a solar 'micronova' being an 'almost inevitable consequence' of the solar system's journey through the Milky Way.

Rapid pole reversals threw climate upside down

A magnetic pole reversal can occur within 80 years (Cal. Berkeley). The current, conclusively established reversal began more than twice as long ago. The planet is now in the "red zone" where this process is accelerating toward a climax. That climax is the final reversal itself, which in the distant past was so sudden and powerful that fossil records have shown animals frozen standing up, and fresh plant remains found in their stomachs.

Some of the many other examples: Tropical coral has been found under Antarctica, proving that the South Pole has not always been in that location. (There are also very old maps showing Antarctica without ice cover). Prehistoric frozen trees on Spitsbergen (Norway) were found to have no rings, and there is only one place on earth where there are no seasons: around the equator. A mile below the Greenland ice sheet, plants belonging to a mild climate have been found, suggesting that the ice there once melted completely. Dinosaur eggs have also been found in the arctic (which is impossible for cold-blooded animals, unless the climate was once very different).

Every 10,000 to 12,000 years an Extinction Level Event

The Pentagon has been aware since 1946 that during a 'magnetic' pole reversal the earth's axis tilts 89 degrees, then 'flips' back over a long period of time. Such a tilt causes not only global cooling and a new ice age, but also enormous geographical changes; mountains are literally torn from their place, and new ones are formed elsewhere. From ice core and soil borings, a cycle of 10,000 to 12,000 years emerges, after which such a polar reversal literally shakes the entire planet to its foundations, and virtually all life is wiped out.

A micronova-whose existence (on numerous stars) is confirmed in the docu by CalTech Dr. August Dunning (ex-NASA, ex-JPL)-can temporarily halt or even reverse the earth's rotation, as described in the Bible and recorded by numerous other ancient cultures. Ancient Peruvian writings speak of a night that lasted 20 hours (while in the Bible, i.e., in Israel, there are accounts of the opposite, i.e., a day that lasted much longer than normal).

A well-known end-time prophecy of the Hopi Indians states that a "blue star" in the sky will announce the end of the present world.

Magnetic field already decreased by at least 20%

The magnetic field has now decreased by at least 20%. The north pole and the south pole (which has now left the continent of Antarctica) are moving toward each other at ever-increasing speed. 'This is not a normal pole shift, but a real reversal,' Davidson continued, pointing out that the decrease is now at least 5% per decade, and the leader of ESA's 'Swarm' mission, Rune Floberghagen, acknowledged this back in 2014 (which cost him his position).

The likely point where the poles will 'collide' is just west of Indonesia (very close to the last point where radar still had contact with flight MH370, before it disappeared without a trace in 2014)

Honorary Ph.D. Professor Dr. James Channell (University of Florida) confirms that the existence of these "magnetic excursions" is now widely recognized in the scientific literature. These magnetic displacements and reversals 'are of very short duration,' and are accompanied by a weakened magnetic field. 'And then you get more powerful UV radiation' on Earth.

'Do governments know more than they tell us?'

Davidson: 'Do the governments of China and the U.S. know more? All the information I share on this channel has been published in major scientific journals, admitting that I have connected these dots myself, and tried to fill in the missing gaps with the resources that researchers have not had in the past. In any case, it seems certain that the CIA figured it out decades ago.'

'It's all about survival, and that's the only good news I can bring to this documentary. Indeed, there is evidence that the population retreated en masse into caves and tunnels. Several times in fact. The fact that we are here now proves that we survived, and returned to the surface.'

That a huge underground network of tunnels and bases was built in the U.S. after World War II, far more complex and larger than the military would ever need, is common knowledge (See these unofficial maps. Incidentally, the existence of many of the underground complexes shown here (presumably only a fraction of what was built) has been confirmed by the government).

Douglas Vogt (Diehold Foundation), who has been writing for years based on censored research that there will be a nova on the sun in 2046: 'The US government knows the sun is going nova, there is no question about that. They just want you not to know... They desperately give every other possible explanation (especially the CO2/climate change hoax - X.) just to keep you from looking at the sun.'

Catastrophism confirmed on earth and in the solar system

Especially since last year, numerous new studies and papers are appearing that are beginning to confirm Davidson's 'catastrophism' theories. Several examples of this are shown in the docu, such as a study by Leiden University (Leiden Observatory) which states that planets can survive even a supernova (let alone a micronova). A year ago, other scientists noted that the length of a day has literally "shortened": the Earth's rotation has increased to the point that in 2020 the 28 shortest days since 1960 were measured. In 2021, that acceleration continued.

In addition to major sudden events on the planets in our solar system (the "dark vortex" on Neptune that has reversed, the 20% decrease in Pluto's atmosphere, and significant chemical (helium) changes in the solar wind), there are also numerous visible signals on Earth, such as the 2 million lightning discharges counted in Michigan last year, one-third more than normal. Similar reports have emerged from locations around the world - such as the Arctic region, where solar energy can enter the atmosphere most easily. Two new types of lightning discharges have also been observed over mountainous regions and in winter storms.

Parts of the animal world are much more sensitive to magnetic changes. For example, in August, orcas near Spain showed unusually aggressive behavior by attacking and damaging boats en masse in waters where they normally rarely go.

Signs and evidence that 'The next End of the World' has arrived

And what of the February 19, 2021 Science article "A Global Climate Crisis 42,000 Years Ago," which argues that we are now in the next crisis (not thanks to human action, but thanks to the sun). The pattern changes point to a climax in just 20 to 30 years (at most). 'Almost every major point in our book 'The Next End of the World' was confirmed or further explored within 6 months. The nearby stars, the planets (for example, a surprisingly high number of Martian quakes were measured), the sun, our own planet, all demand our attention.'

Last year we saw extraordinary auroras, large landslides (for which people tried to blame farmers), evidence that the brightness of the neighboring star of Barnard was changed not by a planet (as previously claimed), but by changes on the star itself, and evidence of superflares from another "neighbor" of the sun, Wolf 359. In the previous decade, we saw similar violent phenomena in the system of Proxima Centauri, the star closest to the Sun (4.2 light years).

Numerous studies suggest that the decreasing magnetic field is already causing major changes in all layers of the atmosphere (such as a rapidly weakening ozone layer), despite the fact that the activity of the sun itself has actually decreased (solar minimum). An EPP (Earth & Planetary Physics) study also directly linked the changes in CO2 to the weakening of the magnetic field, the REAL cause of 'climate change'.

(Interesting side note: according to a new study, the amount of water under the top layer of the Earth's crust is unimaginably greater than previously thought. This could explain where the water from the Flood went).

Scientists 'now know what's coming'

What is the reason that Davidson's catastrophism models, waved away for years, are now suddenly being studied so widely and seriously, and confirmed (in whole or in part) by absolute top scientists and major research institutions? 'Two answers. One: more and more scientists are seeing the light and starting to get it. I am in weekly contact with dozens of them, working at numerous universities and organizations. They know what's coming. They know what they can publish now. There is overwhelming recognition now.'

'The second reason is you. You are bringing about these changes.' Researchers and journals became interested as larger and larger numbers of people wanted to know more about this topic, started watching the videos en masse, reading the studies about it, and sharing the information with each other and others.

To 5% decrease per year = the end between 2025 and 2030, possibly even earlier

A NASA simulation shows how the so-called L-shells (the smaller magnetic fields that extend to lower altitudes, the lowest of which has decreased by 500 kilometers in just one year) will react to a super solar storm.

Davidson: "That's going to be fun on Earth, isn't it? Moreover, more and more studies in authoritative journals are confirming that polar reversals do not occur silently (as was long claimed), but are actually always E.L.E.'s: Extinction Level Events. 'While we are all screaming about Covid and climate change, THIS is now going on worldwide. People, we are in big trouble. Remember that official science now says that once it happens, it happens FAST - almost 100 times faster than NASA's 5% per century.

'That's extraordinarily extreme, and amounts to 5% decline per year, so 1% every 72 days. It then takes several years at best, and that's no joke. At 5% per decade, we are already at a 20% or more reduction. And if the magnetic field accelerates again, that is very bad news. It is very likely that in 2019 and 2020 (during a 'geomagnetic shock' identified by Swarm) that acceleration has indeed already occurred.'

The point at which the various colored lines split is where we are now. 'My absolute best estimate is that we will end up somewhere between the orange and green line.' That's between 2030 and 2046. Note: that's when the absolute end is - the collapse of civilization begins (much) sooner, presumably many years, especially since our society has become so dependent on electricity and the weakening field (at -50%? maybe -30%?) will no longer be able to protect our systems. That places the potential end of our civilization possibly as early as (or even shortly before) 2025. With any luck, we have a few more years.

Of course, this will never be officially announced because it would cause mass panic. Chances are that it will be called a "conspiracy theory" (and the blame will be shifted to the CO2/climate change hoax) for as long as it takes, until the huge impact is undeniable.

The elite dig in or have escape to space

Since 2020 and 2021, everyone with a still functioning brain is rebelling against everything that is being done now (corona plandemic, Agenda-2030, Great Reset, Green New Deal, etc.) to totally control humanity and keep it away from the truth. That truth, by the way, is well known to the elite; not for nothing is the world's richest man, Jeff Bezos, near his launch pad in Texas, hollowing out a mountain to hide in once cosmic disaster hits our planet.

And why is Elon 'Tesla' Musk so preoccupied with exactly the same things: digging tunnels, or just an escape to space? The number of billionaires and celebrities (George Clooney, Lady Gaga, Kim Kardashian, among others) preparing to buy and have survival bunkers constructed (which, of course, they do not literally call them that) is rapidly increasing. 'In what

they do you see what you would do if you had their
money, and knew what was coming.'

'Eyes open, no fear,' Davidson ends all his videos.
Historically, such a cataclysmic disaster is survivable (or
we wouldn't be here now), but it will be very few. In
addition to a lot of costly and strenuous preparation
and accumulation of knowledge and techniques to
survive without electricity, you also need to have an
escape route to a space deep underground, where you
should be able to stay safe for quite some time. For 99%
of humanity, that is not realistic anyway, especially
since there will be no time left to make and execute
drastic decisions once everything starts.

**Ancient prophecies foretell exactly what is about to
happen**

Believers and connoisseurs of the Bible should not be
surprised, for numerous prophecies foretell everything
described in this article:

'But the day of the Lord will come like a thief. In that
day the heavens will pass away with noise, and the
elements will perish with fire, and the earth and the
works upon it will be found. (2 Peter 3:10)

"I will make mortals rarer than purified gold and men
than fine gold of Ofir. Therefore I will cause the heavens
to falter, and the earth to tremble from its place
because of the wrath of the Lord of hosts, in the days of
his burning wrath. (Isaiah 13:12-13)

'And the heavens receded like a scroll being rolled up, and every mountain and island was torn from its place. And the kings...and superiors...and rich and powerful and every slave and free hid themselves in the dens and rocks of the mountains...' (Revelation 6:14-15)

'For thus says the Lord of hosts: 'A moment yet, a short while, then I will make heaven and earth, the sea and the dry land tremble.' (Haggai 2:7)

'The earth bursts wide open, the earth shakes violently, the earth staggers terribly; the earth staggers greatly like an inebriated man, and sways to and fro like a nightshade; for her transgression weighs heavily upon her; she falls and does not rise again.' (Isaiah 24:19-20)

'Yea, trembling shall be before Me the fish of the sea, the fowl of the heavens, the beasts of the field, and all the creeping beasts that creep upon the earth, and all men that live upon the earth; the mountains shall fall, the mountain walls shall fall, every wall shall fall to the earth.' (Ezekiel 38:20)

Escape from this, however, the elite can forget, but there is hope

'And it shall come to pass, that he who flees from the terrifying noise shall fall into the pit, and he who climbs out of the pit shall be caught in the snare; yea, the floodgates in the high shall be opened, and the foundations of the earth shall tremble.' (Isaiah 24:18)

'Well then, ye rich, weep and mourn over the calamities that shall befall you. Your wealth is rotten...your gold and silver is rusty, and the rust of it will testify against you and consume your flesh like fire. Thou hast gone to lay up treasures, while these are the last days... thou hast lived sumptuously on earth and indulged thyself... thou hast condemned the righteous, yea killed them; there is no defence against thee.' (James 5:1-6)

'In those days it will come to pass, that the Lord will bring visitation... upon the kings of the earth upon the face of the earth. And they shall be gathered together, as prisoners are gathered into a pit, and shut up in a dungeon; and after many days they shall be visited.' (Isaiah 24:21-22)

However, there is also hope, for the cycle now appears to be coming to a definite end. There will not be another 12,000-year period until the next ELE:

'Then His voice caused the earth to totter, but now He has given a promise, saying: Once more I will not only shake the earth, but also the heavens. This, once more, refers to the changing of faltering things, as of something merely created, that what is not faltering may remain. (Hebrews 12:26-27)

'And I saw a new heaven and a new earth, for the first heaven and the first earth had passed away... and He will wipe away all tears from their eyes, and death shall be no more, neither shall there be mourning, nor crying, nor trouble any more, for the first things have passed away. And He that sat upon the throne said, Behold, I make all things new. (Revelation 21)

The promised final redemption therefore seems imminent, but until then we will have to brace ourselves and persevere - quite apart from the fact that our own 'kings' are busy with their policies to make our lives a real hell in the years to come.

Legal euthanasia?

Human life is being valued less and less at a rapid pace
- What is the matter with humanity, that a death cult is followed so massively?

The New Zealand Ministry of Health has confirmed that Covid-19 is a legal reason to commit euthanasia, and that doctors may decide for themselves whether to cooperate. Earlier this month, Switzerland was in the news for a developed suicide capsule, which - contrary to media reports - has not yet been approved.

An even more worrying sign that a true death cult is now being followed around the world is the astonishing fact that very few people seem to care about the millions of Covid-vax victims (dead, disabled and sick) that have been killed in barely a year. In fact, the call for everyone to be mandatorily given these life-threatening injections is growing louder, especially in politics.

In response to a WOB request from New Zealand's The Defender in November, asking whether Covid-19 patients are eligible for euthanasia, the Ministry of Health responded that granting such a request is "determined on a case-by-case basis. Therefore, the ministry cannot make definitive statements about who is eligible. In some circumstances, a person with Covid-19 may be eligible for assisted suicide.'

One of the important criteria for euthanasia in New Zealand is that the applicant in question himself or herself experiences his or her suffering as intolerable. Further, there must be a 'terminal illness', but certainly in view of events since 2020, the interpretation of who is 'terminal' has become particularly loose when a run-of-the-mill respiratory virus with a flu-like IFR of only 0.15% (0.05% to age 70) was (and still is) extremely overhyped as a life-threatening 'killer virus'.

'Door wide open for abuse'

DefendNZ therefore believes that the vague and broad criteria of the Euthanasia Act passed in 2020 'opened the door wide for abuse', and the 'Covid-19 pandemic' has become potentially 'even more dangerous' as a result. Incidentally, the New Zealand figures also show the opposite of 'dangerous': since the end of March, 51 Covid deaths have been recorded, out of a population of 5 million = 0.001% . For comparison, 239 people died in traffic in the same period).

Although it is not directly described as such, that abuse is obvious: it has now become a lot easier for doctors, under the guise of Covid-19, to put to sleep people who have been falsely convinced by all the propaganda that they are suffering from a very serious disease. Possibly even worse, it could theoretically cover up vaccine victims.

Suicide capsule

The fact that human life is rapidly being considered worth less and less Is also demonstrated by a suicide capsule built in Switzerland. The 3D printed "Sarco" was developed by Exit International and euthanasia activist Philip "Dr. Death" Nischke, and was designed by Alexander Bannink. A person who wants to end their life can have the capsule placed in a favorite spot, sit in it, and then with the push of a button have the capsule filled with nitrogen. The person falls asleep after about 30 seconds and dies a (reportedly) painless death within minutes.

Contrary to what many media reported, this suicide capsule, which can immediately be used as a coffin after death, has not yet been approved by the Swiss authorities. However, trials with it will be undertaken starting in 2022.

For years, Switzerland has been an increasingly popular destination for foreigners who want to leave life "without a hitch. The Alpine country has no special euthanasia law, but has such broad laws and regulations that it is not forbidden. Last year about 1,300 people ended their earthly existence in Switzerland.

Human life is rapidly becoming less valuable

The world thus seems to be moving step by step in the direction of the science fiction novel 'Logan's Run' (1967), which was filmed in 1976 and deals with a future society in which resources and consumption are strictly regulated by compulsory euthanasia of everyone who reaches the age of 30. At the moment, 'Logan's Run' is still a long way off, but recent history shows that a lot can change in a very short time. In 2009, swine flu vaccines were withdrawn in the U.S. after 'only' 25 deaths, in part because of the intense public and media reaction to this.

By the end of 2021, officially almost 1,000 times as many Americans have died from the Covid injections, and a multitude have suffered serious (often permanent) health damage, yet politicians, media and a large part of the public are all pushing for these 'kill shots' to be made mandatory. The (indirect) killing or damaging of a fellow human being has apparently suddenly become a lot more acceptable.

In the EU, according to the official database EudraVigilance, on December 18, the counter stood at 34,337 Covid vax deaths and 3,120,439 wounded, of which about half were serious and/or permanent (including autoimmune disorders and disabilities such as lost limbs, blindness, deafness, etc.) (3). Since the Netherlands accounts for 21% of the reports, that would amount to 7210 compatriots who have died from a Covid-19 'vaccination' since the beginning of this year.

Suicide capsule

The fact that human life is rapidly being considered worth less and less is also demonstrated by a suicide capsule built in Switzerland. The 3D printed "Sarco" was developed by Exit International and euthanasia activist Philip "Dr. Death" Nischke, and was designed by Alexander Bannink. A person who wants to end their life can have the capsule placed in a favorite spot, sit in it, and then with the push of a button have the capsule filled with nitrogen. The person falls asleep after about 30 seconds and dies a (reportedly) painless death within minutes.

Contrary to what many media reported, this suicide capsule, which can immediately be used as a coffin after death, has not yet been approved by the Swiss authorities. However, trials with it will be undertaken starting in 2022.

For years, Switzerland has been an increasingly popular destination for foreigners who want to leave life "without a hitch. The Alpine country has no special euthanasia law, but has such broad laws and regulations that it is not forbidden. Last year about 1,300 people ended their earthly existence in Switzerland.

Human life is rapidly becoming less valuable

The world thus seems to be moving step by step in the direction of the science fiction novel 'Logan's Run' (1967), which was filmed in 1976 and deals with a future society in which resources and consumption are strictly regulated by compulsory euthanasia of everyone who reaches the age of 30. At the moment, 'Logan's Run' is still a long way off, but recent history shows that a lot can change in a very short time. In 2009, swine flu vaccines were withdrawn in the U.S. after 'only' 25 deaths, in part because of the intense public and media reaction to this.

By the end of 2021, officially almost 1,000 times as many Americans have died from the Covid injections, and a multitude have suffered serious (often permanent) health damage, yet politicians, media and a large part of the public are all pushing for these 'kill shots' to be made mandatory. The (indirect) killing or damaging of a fellow human being has apparently suddenly become a lot more acceptable.

In the EU, according to the official database EudraVigilance, on December 18, the counter stood at 34,337 Covid vax deaths and 3,120,439 wounded, of which about half were serious and/or permanent (including autoimmune disorders and disabilities such as lost limbs, blindness, deafness, etc.) (3). Since the Netherlands accounts for 21% of the reports, that would amount to 7210 compatriots who have died from a Covid-19 'vaccination' since the beginning of this year.

When was the last time so many people were killed (either directly or with a 'delay') by the active actions of other people? We have to go back to the Second World War, when there were approximately 250,000 victims, including soldiers and more than 100,000 Jews.

Millions of deaths hardly make an impact

Officially, we are nowhere near that number (yet), but consider that a few years ago, after extensive statistical research, it was determined that the EudraVigilance database reflects only 6% of the actual number of victims. The American VAERS database does even worse at 1%. This gives you a more accurate picture of the massive carnage that is going on right now, but that almost no one seems to really care about, especially in politics (with a few exceptions).

Now that there appears to have been no excess mortality at all last year, and the number of hospital/IC admissions was lower than in the previous 7 years, over 7,200 people have therefore been given a death stimulus, completely pointlessly. (Quite apart from the question of whether such a shot is ever useful or wise). All of these people could and should have lived. Prickly pity" was voted "word of the year" by a huge majority, but where are the protests? Where is the popular anger? Even among the 'awake' section I detect a sometimes disconcerting resignation about this.

Entrepreneurial analyst Erik Boosma is one of those who does feel shocked about this. At the beginning of December he converted the official EU statistics into the most likely real figures, and in 11 months' time arrived at the staggering number of 6.2 million vax deaths worldwide - more than the number of Jews murdered during the Holocaust. And that's for a so-called "pandemic" that, even according to the world-renowned British Medical Journal, exists only on TV and the corona dashboard.

What is going on with humanity?

What on earth (seriously!) is going on with humanity? How can so many have allowed themselves to be so easily frightened to death, and so readily agree to what is effectively a worldwide death cult, complete with heavenly atrocities such as the injection of children, who themselves have ZERO risk of serious illness and death from Covid, but who have now been shown to suffer greatly from these life-threatening gene-manipulation injections?

Isn't this even worse than the attitude of the German people during the 30's and 40's, for whom it was a lot easier to look the other way because the mass murders by the Nazis took place mostly out of sight and behind barbed wire, and also involved specific (ethnic, religious and social) 'target groups'?

A collective mass hypnosis and psychosis seems to have taken hold of the majority of the world's population. Humanity and empathy turned out to be a wafer-thin layer of civilization, which disappeared like snow in the sun at the slightest breeze and made way for fear and extremely selfish (and totally misplaced) self-preservation, which with false terms such as 'only together' is presented as a new 'virtue' in which everyone has to participate in order to be 'accepted' and to retain their freedom.

A planet full of monsters

I don't know how you experience it, but on the threshold of 2022 I personally can do little else than conclude that I appear to live on a planet full of unscrupulous monsters, who try to hunt down the few that still have some light in them, and in time will also want to clear them out.

No, that's not an uplifting message so close to a new year - and I'm very happy to be proven wrong on this one! -but regular readers certainly know by now that I am averse to sweet talk, velvet gloves, pretexts and empty 'behind-the-clouds-sunshine' optimism. If you prefer that, there are more than enough other sites, writers, journalists and commentators for it.

If you can take it, brace yourself, because tomorrow's planned year-end article will contain an even tougher - and scientifically based - message.

Call the authorities?

In Germany, a help center for family and friends of conspiracy theorists has been set up, supposedly because the latter group would put great strain on relationships with their dissenting views. The only problem is that the truth is demonstrably slightly different: it is precisely the 'conspiracy theorists' who have been proved right time and time again, and it is their family and friends who have mentally succumbed to the constant propaganda from the government and mainstream media, thus completely losing sight of reality. Rather, therefore, there should be a point of help for these gullible people, complete with the same kind of program that former cultists are treated with to restore their brainwashed thinking.

'Colleagues, friends or family who can miss the vaccines like a toothache or see the hand of Bill Gates or Georges Soros in everything.... 'Conspiracy theorists see every development in the pandemic as part of a larger plan,' writes the Belgian Standard. This puts such a strain on friendships and relationships that in Potsdam (Berlin) the Demos-Institut für Gemeinwesenberatung has now been set up, officially to restore ties between believers and non-believers.

This could theoretically be done in a much simpler way, for example if the Covax sect members would check how many times in the last 2 years alone the mainstream media have been wrong, and their "conspiracy-thinking" relatives and friends have been right.

Depopulation as yet unproven

By far the biggest unproven 'conspiracy theory' is that the injections are part of a depopulation program to reduce the world's population to a maximum of 1.5 billion people (Agenda-2030). The 'vaccines' are said to be purposely designed so that they will do maximum damage and kill billions only after 2 to 3 years.

Ofcourse I will continue to hope and pray that it remains a theory, but so far more and more is pointing to the fact that it could become reality in the coming years. Numerous scientists, doctors and experts have been warning for some time that an unimaginable mass slaughter by the injections is certainly not inconceivable. Even WHO-European Advisory Group of Experts in Immunization ex-VP Professor Christian Personne has literally warned that "It is not unvaccinated people who are dangerous, but vaccinated people. These are a danger to others and should be quarantined if they do not want to become seriously ill.'

New rule of thumb: The opposite of what you are told is usually true

If there is one thing that people with a shred of remaining independent and critical thinking capacity have seen confirmed time and time again since 2020, it is that the mainstream media cannot be trusted for one second anymore and are merely spreading state propaganda, and in doing so have become the biggest conspiracy promoters themselves. Promoters, because the reality of these 'conspiracies' can simply be read back in official publications of, for example, the World Eocnomic Forum, the United Nations (/WHO) or the European Union.

The conspiracy-promoting newspapers and Tv channels have even descended to 'Bidens Rule': if he says 'blue', you can almost be sure it will be 'red'. If he predicts heat, get out your winter coat. If he insists that something is 'nonsense' or a 'conspiracy', take it very seriously because it is most likely the truth. And when the NOS tries to scare you to death about a common respiratory virus to get you to 'take the shot', you can breathe a sigh of relief because by now you have experienced that the truth is in almost all cases the exact opposite of what 'the screen' tries to make you believe.

In fact, we have a very predictable and 'reliable' dictator at the head of the country, who seems to have copied his psychological methods of population manipulation directly from Saul Alinksy's 'Rules for Radicals'. So just reverse everything he says, and you can hardly be wrong.

The reckoning of 2022

Top economist Martin Armstrong: 'It will NEVER get back to normal, and it would be nice if we had until 2024 at all before political chaos topples the financial system' = 'When you pit groups against each other a civilization collapses'

We wrote recently that the current "plague Christmas" lockdown has nothing to do with public health at all, but with the imminent collapse of the ECB. The lockdown is only intended to psychologically 'train' people for a period when ATMs will be locked, their bank accounts will no longer be accessible and they will be forced to stay at home. An equally important reason is that the governments want to point to the supposed (in any case harmless) virus variant Omicron as the 'culprit' of the impending crisis, which they want to use to push through their dream federal European superstate. Either way, 2022 will be the year when the reckoning for the EU's years of failed financial-economic policies begins. The pain that this crisis will cause will, of course, once again be passed on to ordinary citizens.

The American top economist Martin Armstrong writes that on the threshold of 2022 we have a 'very serious look' at the economic crisis resulting from the sovereign debt crisis in Europe. 'I have been warning for 10 years that the situation would become critical, and have been at meetings with many central banks during this period to warn them that governments cannot continue to borrow money indefinitely with no intention of ever paying it back.'

Covid-19 pretext to cover up upcoming default

'The Day of Reckoning has come,' he observes. 'They have used Covid-19 to create panic, just to get to the point where their solution is a default (bankruptcy) that will be disguised as a rescue for the people.'

This is therefore the real reason why one of the pillars of the economy, the hospitality sector (and with it numerous related sectors), is now being deliberately destroyed at an accelerated pace by the Western regime with a completely pointless lockdown. Our economy MUST first be destroyed to enable the 'Great Reset' (/ 'Build Back Better') coup of the WEF, of which Sigrid Kaag was (/ is) shown to be one of the main executors.

Earlier this month, the Netherlands, Israel, the US with 7 other countries plus the IMF, the BIS and the World Bank practiced on the (false flag) cyber attack on the financial system announced by the WEF. A possible days- or even weeks-long blackout - for which possibly Russia will be blamed - will be used as a pretext for an attempt at a completely digital reboot of the system, in which all forms of property (including financial) and every say, participation and freedom of citizens and companies will be taken away forever and will fall under total control of central banks and governments.

'Would be nice if we have until 2024 at all'

'I report on the true state of the global financial system, and for most it may be shocking,' Armstrong continued. 'It's not a matter of simple hyperinflation, because that implies that a currency will still survive.' In other words, the debt crisis now unfolding is so severe and unsolvable that even the survival of the currencies themselves (such as the euro in Europe and the dollar in the US) is at stake. That means that our current prosperity will also take very big hits.

'The real prospect is totally different from the assertions of the leaders who have been telling the same story for decades since the collapse of Bretton Woods. Those in power are already coming up with stories of armed revolution if Trump does not win in 2024 **. It would be nice if we had that long at all, before political chaos topples the financial system.'

(** But even his eventual return will not bring relief - quite the opposite. After all, Trump proclaims the same lying 'vax' narrative as the current clique who are supposedly his enemies.)

'When you pit groups against each other a civilization collapses'

'There will NEVER be a return to normal. These people have divided the people on the basis of race and politics (and also on the basis of ethnicity, ancestry, identity, opinion, and as of this year, even medical status). The key to civilization is that people come together when it benefits them ALL. If you start dividing people and pitting one group against another, a civilization collapses.

And in a collapsing civilization is exactly what awaits us between now and 2025 if the common people do not very quickly say massively NO to this communist 'Great Reset' / Agenda-2030 and all that goes with it, of which a digital QR code ID coupled with a 'subscription' to mandatory gene manipulation injections in order to continue to have access to society is by far the most evil, harmful and shameful thing ever imposed on so many people in all of history.

Iran wants your attention?

Massive military exercises in Iran on Israeli attack and ground operation - Head of Iranian Atomic Energy Agency acknowledges country working on offensive nuclear arsenal

With a special "Christmas message," Iran has responded to the recent open announcements by top Israeli military officials and politicians that an attack on Iran's nuclear facilities must come no matter what. A salvo of ballistic missiles was fired from the south of Iran, destroying a replica of Israel's nuclear power plant near Dimona some 1,700 kilometers away. The "Christmas message" is clear: in the event of a military attack, we will cause a nuclear disaster in your little country.

After weeks of lobbying again at the White House and the Pentagon, the Israeli political and intelligence summit seems to have turned a corner. Reports now suggest that the Americans are considering using the stalled negotiations with Iran as an opportunity to give Israel the green light and the desired - and necessary - military support for the attack on Iran's nuclear facilities that Jerusalem has wanted for at least 15 years.

Nuclear disaster in case of full hit on reactor

Although the Iranian armed forces are no match for Israel and the U.S. in material and qualitative terms, the Shi'ite regime in Tehran does hold a major trump card: it has used the delaying tactics used for years during negotiations to build a huge arsenal of missiles, which are now much more accurate than in the past. While Israel has the successful Iron Dome defense system, it is designed for short-range projectiles, and in an overwhelming attack with hundreds of missiles at once can only intercept a small fraction.

The David's Sling missile defense system, which came into service in 2017, was designed to stop ballistic missiles, among other things, but has barely proven itself in practice. Moreover, because of the high cost, Israel will not have deployed hundreds or thousands of them.

The Iranian threat to destroy the nuclear power plant near Dimona will therefore be taken very seriously. Although the plant is hardened to withstand large impacts, there is a risk that a series of hits could still release nuclear material, which could spread across the country depending on the wind direction, or end up over Jordan, Egypt or Saudi Arabia.

With a special "Christmas message," Iran has responded to the recent open announcements by top Israeli military officials and politicians that an attack on Iran's nuclear facilities must come no matter what. A salvo of ballistic missiles was fired from the south of Iran, destroying a replica of Israel's nuclear power plant near Dimona some 1,700 kilometers away. The "Christmas message" is clear: in the event of a military attack, we will cause a nuclear disaster in your little country.

After weeks of lobbying again at the White House and the Pentagon, the Israeli political and intelligence summit seems to have turned a corner. Reports now suggest that the Americans are considering using the stalled negotiations with Iran as an opportunity to give Israel the green light and the desired - and necessary - military support for the attack on Iran's nuclear facilities that Jerusalem has wanted for at least 15 years.

Nuclear disaster in case of full hit on reactor

Although the Iranian armed forces are no match for Israel and the U.S. in material and qualitative terms, the Shi'ite regime in Tehran does hold a major trump card: it has used the delaying tactics used for years during negotiations to build a huge arsenal of missiles, which are now much more accurate than in the past. While Israel has the successful Iron Dome defense system, it is designed for short-range projectiles, and in an overwhelming attack with hundreds of missiles at once can only intercept a small fraction.

The David's Sling missile defense system, which came into service in 2017, was designed to stop ballistic missiles, among other things, but has barely proven itself in practice. Moreover, because of the high cost, Israel will not have deployed hundreds or thousands of them.

The Iranian threat to destroy the nuclear power plant near Dimona will therefore be taken very seriously. Although the plant is hardened to withstand large impacts, there is a risk that a series of hits could still release nuclear material, which could spread throughout the country depending on the direction of the wind, or end up over Jordan, Egypt or Saudi Arabia.

Iran practices on Israeli attack

The destruction of the nuclear reactor replica seemed to be a culmination of days of massive exercises by Iran's Revolutionary Guards on a possible Israeli attack, including the landing of ground troops. At the same time, the state-owned Kayhan newspaper announced that in the event of an attack, Iran would immediately scale up uranium enrichment to 90%, which is sufficient to build nuclear weapons.

The "Iranian Bomb" is exactly what Israel, the US and also ally Saudi Arabia want to prevent. General McKenzie, head of US Central Command, warned in late November that Iranian uranium is now enriched to 60%, and the mullahs in Tehran are "very close this time" to the decision to build a nuclear bomb. Despite this, the country has yet to show a tech that could make such a bomb small enough to be mounted on a missile.

Head of Iranian Atomic Energy Agency acknowledges existence of nuclear weapons program

For years it has been claimed that Iran's nuclear weapons program is a hoax, but the openly acknowledged enrichment of uranium to 60% - completely unnecessary for civilian purposes - and the threat to increase it to 90%, is proof enough in itself. And what about the recent admission by the head of the Iranian Atomic Agency, Fereydun Abbasi-Davani, that the head of the nuclear program, Mohsen Fakrizadeh, who was assassinated last year (most likely by the Mossad), had set up "a nuclear weapons system for offensive purposes," which will also be built without him.

Why can the rest have nuclear weapons, but not us?

Iran's position can be briefly summarized: why are our enemies America (thousands) and Israel (80 to 200 pieces), as well as neighboring Pakistan (110 pieces) allowed to have nuclear weapons, and not us? Objectively, there is little to argue with, especially considering that other countries in the region also have nuclear weapons (Russia, China, India) or are working on them (Turkey, Saudi Arabia).

Could it have something to do with the fact that Iran is a major oil/gas producer that refuses to submit to the Western/Arab alliance, but is in fact an ally of Russia and China? Incidentally, it should be noted that Moscow and Beijing will probably not be waiting for the Iranian bomb either; that would make the Middle East an even more unpredictable and dangerous region than it already is, not least because of the more or less apocalyptic theological ideology espoused by the religious leaders in Tehran.

Still, it can be wondered what exactly an eventual Iranian nuclear bomb will change. After all, using this bomb means an absolutely certain suicide. It therefore seems that Iran, like North Korea, wants to have nuclear weapons primarily as a deterrent.

War seems a matter of time now that influential Americans are in favor

Since the United States lives from conflict and war (the Americans have a higher defense/security budget than all other countries combined), and the infamous 'Project for a new American Century' already identified Iran as one of the targets of a series of wars, it is starting to look like this planned war against Iran is going to happen no matter what.

Some influential American (ex) politicians, such as former Secretary of Defense Leon Panetta and General David Petraeus (who led the Iraq/Aghanistan wars and was also director of the CIA) and the well-known former Middle East diplomat Dennis Ross are now openly calling on the White House to take military action. The Biden administration, however, does not seem to have reached that point yet.

It is to be hoped, by the way, that it never comes to that, especially since such a war could quickly get out of hand and again claim huge numbers of innocent civilian victims. After being lured into all kinds of bloody but pointless wars (Iraq, Afghanistan, Libya, Syria) by Washington (and Brussels) under false pretences, this kind of so-called "preventive" destruction should be over for good.

MAD least bad option

In the absence of the will and confidence to bring about real peace, MAD - Mutual Assured Destruction - still seems to be the least bad option at this moment to prevent countries from fighting and killing each other again. It is precisely the unbalancing of MAD, as the US/NATO is now doing against Russia via Ukraine, that makes another massacre inevitable at some point.

Purely from this point of view, perhaps a few Iranian nuclear bombs could act as a sufficient deterrent to dissuade the aggressive Americans and their allies from yet another military adventure, which no one is really waiting for at all.

At the same time, the top Shi'ite clerics in Tehran may then begin to moderate their tone against Israel. If you bark and threaten for years at an opponent who has already had to fight several existential wars in his short existence, then at a certain moment you provoke a reaction. A reaction, which after some 15 years of repeated Israeli propaganda that 'Iran will have a nuclear bomb in a few months or weeks', now seems to have come very close indeed.

93

Financial 'Third World War' begun: US to raise interest rates, Europe 'doomed'

Yesterday an utterly idiotic and diametrically harsh lockdown was declared from a public health perspective, the next blow dealt by the Western regime in the deliberate step-by-step dismantling of the free and prosperous society and economy. But what is the real motive, aside from implementing the World Economic Forum's communist 'Great Reset' / 'Build Back Better' agenda? It is the impending financial crash we have been writing about for years.

Indeed, the ECB is in serious crisis, and in the worst shape of all central banks. Now that the Americans have unleashed a financial 'Third World War' with announced interest rate hikes, it will be over and done with for the Eurozone and thus the EU from 2022 onwards.

The ECB begged the US Federal Reserve not to raise interest rates, writes the American top economist Martin Armstrong. The Bank of England (BoE) is in much better shape than the ECB, 'which is on the verge of collapse.' The BoE was the first major central bank to raise interest rates from a historic low of 0.1% to 0.25% since the start of the corona pandemic.

'Europe is doomed'

The ECB says it will continue to wind down its government bond purchases, but Armstrong says that is questionable.... 'The ECB is in serious trouble,' because while the Fed did put an end date on its previous purchases, the ECB has continued to hold and buy everything indefinitely. 'Europe is simply doomed,' Armstrong continued accordingly. 'The lockdowns that Schwab's Great Reset agenda according to make claims of economic growth a very bad joke.'

'The ECB is in a serious crisis. The BoE didn't follow the course of the ECB, so it's not in a state that it needs to be in intensive care.' His unique A.I. Socrates had already foreseen it: more interest rate hikes are coming in 2022.

The ECB already introduced zero/negative interest rates in 2014 to keep the euro afloat at all costs (= at the expense of SMEs and citizens (pensions/purchasing power)). Therefore, the bank simply CANNOT raise interest rates without causing a financial-economic mega-crash, which will wipe out hundreds of thousands of companies and millions of jobs, and bring most EU states to the brink of state bankruptcy (or even push them over it).

The crash that will wipe out everything

But the alternative that the planners in Brussels and Frankfurt seem to have chosen, and which as usual is slavishly followed by The Hague, will cause a different kind of mega-crash that will certainly be no less painful -

quite the opposite. The years of zero/negative interest rate policy has driven away just about all foreign investors, has effectively drained the west europes pension funds (the richest in the EU), and has undermined the value of the euro and our purchasing power.

The interest rate hikes will cause capital to flee even faster to the US and Great Britain. The last bit of confidence in the euro will disappear completely, and the ECB can only compensate the depreciation of everything by unlimitedly printing (digital) money. Result: sky-high inflation and a deep depression with disappearing services and large-scale shortages of food, energy and goods, resulting in widespread poverty.

One blunder after another

What should have been done? First, it was already a capital blunder to introduce the euro at all (2000/2002). Critics who warned of the serious consequences in the 1990s appear to have been proved right about everything.

Second, the Eurozone should have been broken up during the financial crisis of 2008-2011, and/or parallel national currencies should have been allowed again. Instead, Mario Draghi's "whatever it takes" was chosen to "save" the euro. That is: to postpone the inevitable demise by x number of years, designed to keep the banks and big financial players afloat.

Default: Citizens and SMEs will be stripped of everything

The motive for the current hard lockdown is that the ECB/EU has always intended to cover up this total failure with a planned 'default' that would erase all debts in one fell swoop. That is why Klaus Schwab bravuraly announced 'you will own nothing': the governments will in fact wipe out all private property, including financial (including pensions). Really EVERYTHING will be confiscated by the state (= central banks). Every form of control and ownership will be taken away from citizens and companies.

After that it is 'bitter poverty and death', as Sven Hulleman aptly described it last year. Because with a UBI (Universal Basic Income) and a CBDC (Central Bank Digital Currency) you might just be able to meet your basic needs, and then only if you have saved up enough social credit points to keep a valid QR code. Savings and free travel are no longer possible anyway.

Democracy ended, elections manipulated

'This is the end of an era,' Armstrong also writes. 'Everyone keeps talking about Covid, the vaccines, the vaxpas and the lockdowns, but Klaus Schwab's real agenda is to end democracy, which they call 'populism' because we are supposedly too stupid to know what is good for us. But all they care about is staying in power... If a fund manager had run his business like the governments, he would have been thrown in jail for 20+ years.'

He therefore warns that the various elections in 2022, 2023 and 2024 (including Australia, US (midterm), France (president), Italy, Great Britain) will be manipulated (just as has most likely been done with elections in the US and various EU countries in recent years). 'For these people and their agenda, the stakes are so high that elections are their biggest risks,' Armstrong continued. 'They need to control those to achieve their end goal.' (2)

With the Emergency Act, democracy was already permanently abolished last year, making it pointless to expect change through this route ever again. The apparent 'resignation' of Biden, which subsequently revealed itself to be a real dictatorship that had no respect for (fundamental) laws and human rights, is rock-solid proof of this.

2022 - 2025

Depending on geopolitical developments (Russia/Ukraine, China) and the purposefully created energy crisis, the time frame in which the coming crash will take place varies from a few weeks to several years. But no matter how short or long it takes, it's going to start in 2022 either way. By 2025, we will no longer recognize our country and continent. ALL of our freedom and much of our prosperity will be gone, and if the vax mortality continues as it is now presumably a substantial part of our population as well. We will by design have been plunged into the harshest and most inhumane totalitarian dictatorship ever.

According to Armstrong's A.I. model, the final collapse of the West will take until 2032. I personally think it won't take that long, but no one can see into the future. Should a hastily federalized EU manage to complete the 'Great Reset' and establish a communist climate-vaccine dictatorship, the final years until the end of our civilization will be nothing short of horrific for everyone. ('The Fourth Turning' and Deagel assume the end in 2025, which seems more likely to me personally).

Grateful?

People like to read something positive, some wrote, and I get that. I'd like that myself. But this is not the time for "tralalala we're going to win" reassurances, only to slump back on the couch and start waiting. It is 1940, the war has just begun, and masses of people are dying. After years of preparation, stigmatization and exclusion, the Holocaust is about to go into effect. Resistance is discouraged, betrayed, arrested and shot. No one knows if the occupation and the war will ever end. Positivity' became primarily 'passivity', except for a very small group of people who, risking life and limb, did become active.

There are people who say they are 'grateful' for the corona crisis and even see it as a 'gift'. Well, if you had used that language in 1940, shortly after the outbreak of World War II, the bombing of Rotterdam and the Nazi occupation of our country, you would probably have been slapped across the face. That's honestly how I feel when I hear someone - albeit well-intentioned - use these kinds of terms. This is not the time for gratitude; this is the time for anger and gathering courage to stand up without violence (because with violence you are going to lose) against the tyranny that is now being imposed on us, before unprecedented numbers of people are directly or indirectly murdered by it.

It's war (and it's being waged against us)

It is war. I repeat: it's war. A globalist climate-vaccination sect driven by the notorious banking families consisting of Big Pharma, Big Tech and Big Finance (BlackRock et al.) through the WHO, WEF, IMF, US/NATO/EU and Vatican, among others, has taken total control of most governments, and has declared war on all forms of freedom, independence, self-determination and personal prosperity and ambitions with the deliberate destruction of our market economy, stable energy and food supply and public health.

Worse still: by the mandatory injection of gene manipulating and body-altering / brain-damaging substances, and the desire to prevent and remove from the atmosphere the lifeblood of all life (CO2, the level of which is still dangerously low), it is a declaration of war on the survival of all human civilization. One would almost begin to think that there is a non-human - and perhaps even supernatural - power behind this that hates humanity enough to want to exterminate most of us, but without destroying the planet itself in the process.

But no, there's no such thing, is there? That's just something for 'conspiracy theorists', some believers and sf/fantasy movies....

Addition 9:55 pm:

Some readers have rightly asked for a clearer explanation of the connection between the lockdown and the ECB/banking crisis. Herewith some too-appropriate paragraphs from our article of October 23, 2020, which also apply perfectly to the current 'hard lockdown' : 'Curfew pure nonsense, is meant to prepare people for banking crisis lockdown'

Apart from the fact that the only truly dangerous 'virus', that of fear and panic, seems to have severely damaged the intellect and the logical reasoning capacity in all layers of the population, there may be another, logical explanation for such a curfew. For example, it is - in addition to the 1.5 meters and the mouth cap obligation - a perfect 'crowd control' tool, and also a test to see how far one can suppress the people with senseless and totally illogical measures before people revolt en masse.

The moment a curfew-lockdown is accepted, it can be gradually extended (e.g. from 11 p.m. to 9 p.m., or even earlier). If the people accept this, and once they have adjusted to it, the threshold for a 'temporary' total curfew will be much lower, and the government can assume that resistance will be very limited - if it ever comes to that in the still very docile Netherlands.

Such a curfew-lockdown will be particularly useful next year, when the hitherto silent but already erupting banking crisis really kicks in. With a curfew, a run on the banks and ATMs is made impossible in advance. We have been writing for years that this new crisis is coming, and that it will most likely be seized upon to completely digitize all payment traffic.

... Already on March 22, in the article "EU decides very soon to implement bank holiday and permanent ban on cash" we asked ourselves whether the corona crisis is not a pretext to save the banks again, and to push through the long planned European banking union. Such a bank union is an absolute necessity for the EU to seize power, and to subject all member states to a federal dictatorship.

The real agenda?

'Poetic Justice'? Governments and administrations that are now betraying their own peoples will themselves be betrayed by the top of the globalist elite - Flashback to the Illuminati card game we discussed at length in 2009, and on which the 'revenge of the people' was predicted.

A New Zealand billionaire is said to have leaked to a service provider the "real plan" of the Covid planemia and the lockdowns: according to the "Ordo ab Chao" (order out of chaos) concept, all peoples are set up against their own governments, parliaments and administrations, to have them deposed and cleaned up by brute force. The intention would be precisely to get both vaccinated and unvaccinated people to unite because of the betrayal of their administrators and representatives, and the enormous damage they have caused. After the governments are deposed, a power vacuum will follow, into which a new global government will jump as the "great savior. Authentic or not, this supposed plan immediately reminds me of the 'Illuminati card game' we covered extensively over 12 years ago.

'As far as the vaccine narrative is concerned, the tide is turning,' the billionaire is said to have told us. 'I was told that over time the vaccine will increase infections and deaths. That billions will die, and people will become enraged and burn down their governments. Their leaders, scientists and media will be hunted down and hanged in the streets. BOTH sides will burn down their governments. The pro-vaxxers, totally betrayed and dying, will rage. So will the non-vaxxers, for what their government has allowed to happen.'

Those who now promote the 'vaccines' will take the hit. 'That's why they're disposable items. Biden is almost dead, Boris Johnson and Macron are suckers... The time in which the mRNA vaccines will do damage is 2 to 3 years. The extent to which the mRNA (injections) have been taken has exceeded their wildest expectations.'

Because of the anarchy that will then have broken out, a new (Masonic (=Illuminati)) world government would begin to restore order in order to be brought in as 'the great savior' ('Ordo ab chao').

There is speculation that some anti-vaxxers belong to this Masonic group, but as yet there is no evidence for this. That Twitter is now allowing videos and posts featuring vax victims anyway is said to be part of 'the real plan'.

Well-known British anti-vax activist arrested after calling for murder of politicians

74-year-old British anti-vax activist Piers Corbyn was arrested in London yesterday after calling on social media to burn down the buildings and offices of parliamentarians. 'We need to get a bit more physical,' Corbyn said in one of his videos. 'It means we have to depose these lying vaccinators and lying parliamentarians. (But) we have to support and welcome all those who have rebelled or voted against Boris, like the Tories who voted against the measures.'

'We need to beat to death those scum who decided to introduce this new fascism. Make a list of them... and if your parliamentarian is one of them, well, I recommend burning them flat, okay? But I can't say that openly, I hope we're not 'on the air'.

Sadiq Khan, the mayor of London, called Corbyn's call for violence "disgusting and dangerous. Home Affairs Minister Priti Patel described the videos as "nauseating," and called for the strongest possible action against the activist, who just last Saturday took part in a demonstration of (tens of) thousands of people protesting yet another lockdown (plans).

Corona plan pandemic devised by world government behind the scenes

The "real plan," coming from this unnamed billionaire in New Zealand, was allegedly leaked on Reddit in early November.

The loose-tongued billionaire said that if the person he told it to ever shared it, they would never have met. At the same time, he laughed about it because no one would believe it anyway.

Behind the scenes, a de facto world government had been operating for years, made up of the 'brightest minds' on the planet, with most members joining voluntarily. Those who refused were 'dealt with'. In short, the plan involves playing governments and their populations off against each other. To do so, global chaos and panic had to be created first. For that purpose, the corona / Covid pandemic was devised.

Because the plan had been so meticulously prepared for so long, billions of "vaccines" could be available in no time for a supposedly newly discovered virus (the production of so many vaccines normally takes many years). These injections should have been presented as the only way out from the very beginning of the p(l)andemic (exactly what we were literally told by the regime in the early 2020s).

To maximize the pain, it was decided that eventually all children should also be injected (and thus damaged or killed).

Current politicians and decision-makers 'mere cannon fodder'

The most interesting 'revelation' was that most governments, scientists and media actually believe they are dealing with a 'safe' and 'effective' treatment against a viral infection. Even Anthony Fauci is said not to be part of the conspiracy, but like the rest is merely 'cannon fodder' who will be surrendered to the angry crowd at some point.

This is not even a strange line of thought, because people in leadership positions who are now blatantly lying and willing to betray and give up their own people are thereby proving themselves to be extremely untrustworthy and corrupt to everyone - including the elite who manage them.

The Covid 'vaccines' have been formulated in such a way that it will take between 2 and 3 years for most of the injuries and deaths to occur (i.e. between the end of 2022 and 2024). The number of victims will be in the billions. Humanity will be decimated, but not before the enraged survivors will have slaughtered all the responsible politicians, scientists and media heads, the billionaire is said to have explained.

Although it would certainly be a form of 'poetic justice' if the globalists, political leaders, people's representatives, scientists and media heads who are now lying to and betraying the people were themselves betrayed, the gross violence that would be 'planned' is not something we should be looking forward to. After all, a violent uprising / revolution historically claims many innocent victims. It could be countered that the number of innocents sacrificed now and in the coming years for this 'Great Reset' climate-vaccination/lockdown agenda threatens to become gigantic, and a backlash will be inevitable.

Illuminati card game

In 2009, we paid extensive attention in several articles to the 1995 'Illuminati card game' which allegedly depicted numerous planned world events. Many of these events appear to have come true in whole or in part by the end of 2021, such as the 9/11 attacks on the Twin Towers (albeit not with a literal 'nuke') and the Pentagon, of which it has been undisputed for years that this was a 'false flag' operation to justify the 'war on terror.

'The Super Plan: the people really win'

Analyst commentator 'G' responds that while this is 'the Plan,' the nations should focus on the 'Super Plan, if the people of the world fight back and actually WIN. Once they gain courage and a will of steel, and use every possible weapon they can find to help this beast to its end.'

The new world that is then built will be based on principles of true freedom and maximum self-determination for each individual, each people and each nation.

There will be no more centrally controlled unions, world organizations, forums and 'united....', no more mega banks, no more multinational corporations, but only decentralized agreements based on voluntary cooperation and respect for each other's borders and cultures.

In short: the exact opposite of the 'Great Reset' and 'Agenda-2030', with which the entire world is now being brought under totalitarian technocratic communist control, in which all forms of freedom, individuality and participation will be definitively done away with for everyone who survives these crises, and all real power will be centralized.

Presumably, it will be decided already in the next few years what our future will look like: will it be this strangling climate-vaccination dictatorship, the harshest and most inhumane regime this planet has ever known, threatening billions of victims? Or will humanity finally stand united against this evil monster of lies, this hate and destruction Beast, and its small club of human representatives who, over the course of the past centuries, have seized all political, financial-economic and military power.

People only need to do one thing to return to normal: Turn off their screens en masse and resume their lives without restrictions - Immunology expert Pierre Capel: Omicron could be salvation for humanity (and is therefore disaster for governments)

The British Medical Journal (BMJ) has long been one of the most authoritative medical journals. All information is carefully screened, leaving absolutely no room for verifiable and unsubstantiated "conspiracy theories. The BMJ published an article last week in which scientists - including the editor-in-chief - actually conclude that the Covid 'pandemic' exists only on TV and the corona dashboard, because the figures and statistics underline time and again that there is nothing extreme going on, especially with the Omicron variant.

To return to normal, people only need to do one thing: turn off their screens (and in our own country, therefore, permanently stop watching mainstream media, and certainly the infamous 'Mark & Hugo Propaganda-Hypnosis Show').

Pandemic and corona dashboards 'endlessly give new fuel to news stories, making the Covid-19 pandemic constantly in the news, even when the threat is low,' write BMJ editor-in-chief Peter Yoshi and Princen University Ph. D. candidate (history) David Robertson in 'The End of the Pandemic will not be televised. 'With this, they could prolong the pandemic by cutting off a sense of closure or a return to pre-pandemic life.'

Pandemic of deception, manipulation, and death fears

An analysis of the past century has shown that previous pandemics, including the infamous Spanish Flu, gradually disappeared from society once people "stopped allowing themselves to be constantly preoccupied by endemic shock figures. In the decades that followed, people continued to live normally, even when there were new flu epidemics with proportionately high(er) death rates.

'Although depictions of epidemics have been made for centuries, Covid-19 is the first with real-time dashboards, which have permeated and structured the public's experience,' the BMJ continues. 'Misled and manipulated to death seem much more appropriate to me personally, as the dashboards are focused on so-called 'infections' based on the totally unsuitable and debunked PCR test for this purpose.

What is happening now with Omicron - a more contagious, but very weak and even welcome mutation that can only give people a cold and provide group immunity within a few weeks - therefore underscores that even the new lockdowns, social distancing and mouthguard duty have nothing at all to do with public health.

Bewilderment at Europe's overreaction

On screen, Omicron looks like a major threat, but the reality is that (as of December 13) there has only been one death worldwide attributed to this new variant, and 99.99% of people only get a slight cold from it - if they notice anything at all. (In principle, this variant could also be a digital fabrication, since colds and flu symptoms are normal in winter).

The South African doctor who first informed the WHO about the Omicron variant told the Western media that he was "astonished" by the overreaction in Great Britain and Europe. Lockdowns at Christmas, travel restrictions, mouthguards, fines and quarantines - for a simple cold? Yet WHO is once again sowing fear with it, and that is because the implementation of the communist 'Great Reset' - Agenda 2030 climate-vaccination coup must not be jeopardized.

Omicron: disaster or rescue?

Professor (em) of experimental immunology Pierre Capel therefore calls Omicron both "a salvation and a disaster. It can be a salvation for humanity, but then it is a disaster for governments. Or it's a salvation for governments, but a disaster for humanity... We're going into lockdown again - Christmas has to break down, but we knew that all along.'

Capel then reveals that the spike from the Omicron variant is quite different from the Alpha and Delta variants, and is a lot more contagious. 'That has huge implications.' Should we be afraid of that, or happy about it? In any case, the statistics show that 'the lockdowns, one and a half meters ('we're not even going to talk about that nonsense') and hand washing don't matter a damn. Omicron will go its way.' But as it turns out, mortality remains very low. 'It turns out that the disease is considerably less severe.'

Prickly wounds are of no use whatsoever

In Africa, Omicron squeezed out Delta in a matter of weeks, and the variant also seems to be spreading at lightning speed in Europe. But it has a preference for the higher airways, the bronchi.

So you get a bronchitis rather than a pneumonia, because in the lower parts of the lungs it doesn't feel very comfortable. So the severity, as far as location is concerned, is not so bad, because the higher airways are much less vulnerable than those delicate alveoli. But apart from that, it's just less pathogenic.'

'Because of those mutations, the puncture makes no sense at all,' Capel continued. 'We knew that all along: against a rapidly mutating respiratory RNA virus, you can't make vaccines. Even someone from the OMT published about that in 2008, that this is indeed the case and that you shouldn't even start.'

'Because of that prick, which offers no protection, people have become super spreaders. But because those Omicron symptoms are so mild, they have no idea

that they are infecting... Or in other words: in no time
Omicron is roaming the Netherlands. Then you do a
lockdown - not that it helps, but then you can ruin
Christmas. With the QR code comes facial recognition
and your bank details, and then they get out where they
want to go.'

'Saving humanity is hardly pathogenic virus'

'So disaster, or salvation? If you look at public health, in
a few weeks we have population immunity. By such an
infection you not only get defence against spike, but
against the whole virus... whereas with that stupid prick
you only give the one spike - which with all its terrible
side effects is very toxic -, which doesn't work because
it often escapes by mutation.

And what does work makes (of vaccinated people)
super-spreaders. In other words: big party!'

'The salvation for humanity is that we very quickly have
a barely pathogenic virus, which really provides
immunity for the rest of your life.' If another variant
comes along next week, your (natural) immunity will
tackle it at 48 points (proteins) (in contrast to the
'vaccine', which only does this at one point). 'And T-cell
immunity hasn't been studied, but you shouldn't
underestimate that either.'

'But it's a "disaster" if we just let it go and use
Ivermectin, and hardly anyone gets sick. Because then
the government's plans don't go through, and that's a

114

disaster for them. But we in their enormous wisdom give them all the power. So we let fear rule again. And just a little prediction: now you still get a recovery certificate when you have recovered, but with this variant everyone gets that. Then the fear and the grip is gone again, so I think that the recovery certificate will be abolished very quickly and the QR code will only apply to the prick.'

'So dear people, don't be so afraid of Omicron, and make sure you can get your hands on the Ivermectin (is strictly suppressed by the Western regime, GPs can get huge fines and customs confiscates 'suspicious' packages, etc.). Along with some zinc and hydroxychloroquine, because that has nothing to do with mutations. Other than that: enjoy life, and fare thee well.'

Novavax

Novavax's new Covid-19 vaccine is being promoted as more traditional and therefore less harmful than the existing 'big four' injections, but is that really the case? Competitor GSK now claims to have developed the very first 'plant based' vaccine. How does that work, and will this new product also skip the normal years of testing, in order to use people 'live' as guinea pigs? Immunology expert Pierre Capel elaborates on Novavax in his latest video, but is clear in his conclusion: 'Omicron is the really good vaccination.'

Population immunity created by mass infection with this barely pathogenic variant is THE solution, according to him.

Novavax does not turn body into spike factory

Novavax is a so-called recombinant vaccine, as Capel explained in a Bitchute video three days ago. 'That means that the genetic information of the (toxic) spike protein is not introduced into your body, but into a (baculo) virus. That is grown in a laboratory on certain (insect) cells (moths - X.). Those cells produce the spike. Big difference between Novavax and the others that are used now: not you make the spike, but the spike is already made and is administered with an adjuvant. So it becomes a fairly classic type of vaccine.'

But which spike is created via that cell culture? That's the Wuhan-Hu-1 spike, with a total of 6 mutations to protect it from degradation in the body and to make it bind well to the ACE2 receptors. 'When you start making it in your body, everywhere that ACE2 receptor is bound and blocked and a lot of things go terribly wrong (as we can see with the Pfizer, Moderna, Janssen shots). In the case of Novavax, it's mixed with adjuvant Matrix-M.' That's nanoparticles made up of cholesterol, phospholipid and Quillaja saponins (soap substances), where the spike is plugged in.

Lockdown prevents NOTHING, least of all Omicron

'This is a standard form of an adjuvant in a vaccine,' Capel continued. 'However, the old Wuhan spike has mutated some 20,000 times. The Omicron variant therefore differs dramatically from this original Wuhan spike (virus). The binding side is completely changed, which makes it much more contagious (70 times faster than Delta), but also much less pathogenic.

This is because Omicron settles in the upper airways (bronchi), and not in the vulnerable alveoli of the lungs. The infection in the lungs is, according to official measurements, even 10 times lower than the Delta variant. When exhaling, Omicron takes a layer of mucus with it, making it very stable and able to remain in the air for a very long time. A lockdown has absolutely nothing to do with this, and prevents NOTHING," underlines the immunology expert. (In short: the Christmas lockdown is nothing but pure bullying, and of the most harmful kind.)

'Omicron the really good vaccine; Novavax barely works against it'

'So Novavax doesn't have any of those horrible side effects, because it spikes outside your body, not in it,' Capel summarizes. 'It has fairly classical adjuvants, and that's what's needed. It also generates T-cell immunity and antibodies in the right amounts. Just because it's an aged spike, it has very little effect on Omicron in a neutralizing sense... If it doesn't help, it doesn't hurt; it may have a little effect, but not crazy much.'

'Omicron is spreading like crazy, and we can be very happy about that because it is much less pathogenic. But Omicron is the really good vaccine. So then you get fine (popular) immunity... Realize that natural immunity to Covid is more than enough and the vaccine is basically unnecessary, and that if you get very sick there is just medication (especially the banned/suppressed Ivermectin). All the bullshit (from the government) that is now so idiotically proposed, we'll talk about that another time.

'I hope this information gives you some peace of mind,' he concludes (1). Perhaps that peace of mind applies a little less to vaxxers, as an official Danish government report (from the Statens Serum Institut) shows that 91% of Omicron 'infections' occur in vaccinated people. Now while Omicron is harmless, it does demonstrate once again the hard truth that the Covid injections not only offer no protection, but in addition weaken and damage the immune system, as has been established in numerous previous studies, and recently confirmed by the UK Health Security Agency.

Novavax less harmless than thought

On April 1, 2021, Novavax R&D president Dr. Gregory Glenn explained to CNN that an intact virus was never used in the development of their vaccine, but only genetic information published on the Internet. 'We never touched the coronavirus itself.' And why not? Because they didn't have the (alleged) virus itself. In other words, you are developing a vaccine against something that you don't even own yourself, but that only exists on paper (in this case, the screen). So how do you know if it works against anything at all?

Bioscientists are also wondering how pure the Novavax is, how many proteins and cell particles from the moth cells remain in the vaccine, and what they might be doing in the human body. And because the injected spike protein has been altered in a number of places to protect it from degradation, it therefore remains floating around in our bodies (much) longer. From the other injections, we now know what enormous damage that has done to millions by now.

(For example, take a look at this official graph: the Covid injections have killed more people in less than a year than all other existing vaccines combined in 30 years. Presenting this as 'safe' is therefore nothing short of criminal:)

Furthermore, the adjuvants used are definitely not that innocuous. Experience with other vaccines shows that many people do not seem to tolerate the soaps and phospholipids used immunologically well. Possibly even more dangerous is the demonstrated fact that nanoparticles spread throughout the body within minutes, as Capel also described in his previous video. This means that these nanoparticles can get into crucial organs, the heart and the brain, with toxic spikes.

In short: the Novavax vaccine does indeed seem less harmful, but it is certainly not necessarily harmless. If it is then considered that it is actually useless against the current variants, and natural immunity is anyway many times better, stronger and more durable, then this vaccine is also completely superfluous.

First plant-based vaccine developed

Actually, the same can be said in advance about the very first 'plant-based' vaccine in the world developed by GSK/Medicago (2). The antigens (virus-like particles) for this as yet unapproved vaccine, tentatively referred to as CoVLP, have been grown in genetically modified crops (such as potatoes and corn).

According to Medicago, which has been working on this technology for 20 years, the advantage is that while the virus-like particles are recognized by the immune system and trigger a response, they do not contain a nucleus of genetic material, are not infectious and cannot replicate.

While clinical trials with some 24,000 adults in 6 countries, which are said to have shown 71% efficacy, have been completed, it normally takes many years to investigate whether a new type of vaccine is "safe" enough to be injected into people on a large scale. The WHO's stated 'almost negligible' risk that the vaccine is contaminated with a plant virus that can damage your health means that there is indeed that chance.

Moreover, again, we are dealing with a drug based on genetically modified cells, and with adjuvants that enter

the human body. And again, we are talking about
supposed "protection" against a respiratory virus that is
statistically no more dangerous than a mild flu and that
mutates at lightning speed, and it is therefore
scientifically impossible to develop a working vaccine
against it (not to mention that the Novavax R&D
president acknowledged not even having that virus in
his hands).